100
THINGS TO DO IN
DENVER
BEFORE YOU
DIE

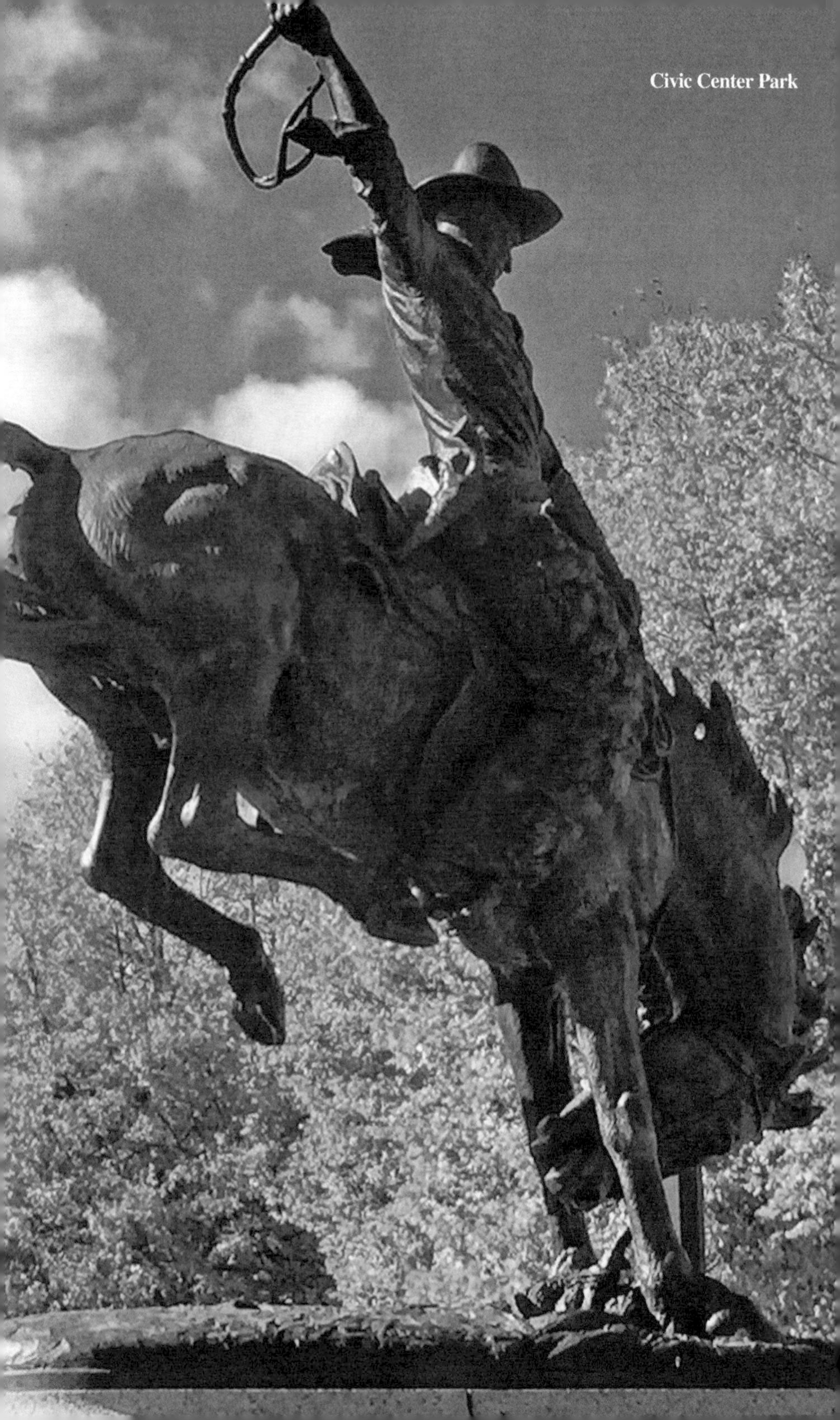
Civic Center Park

100

THINGS TO DO IN
DENVER
BEFORE YOU
DIE

RICH GRANT AND IRENE RAWLINGS

REEDY PRESS

Library of Congress Control Number: 2015957512

ISBN: 9781681060309

Design by Jill Halpin

Cover Photo: Stevie Crecelius for VISIT DENVER

Printed in the United States of America
16 17 18 19 20   5 4 3 2 1

Please note that websites, phone numbers, addresses, and company names are subject to change or cancellation. We did our best to relay the most accurate information available, but due to circumstances beyond our control, please do not hold us liable for misinformation. When exploring new destinations, please do your homework before you go.

CONTENTS

● ●

Music and Entertainment

• •

Sports and Recreation

• •

Culture and History

● ●

• •

PREFACE

One of the worst movies ever made was 1995's *Things to Do in Denver When You're Dead*. It starred Andy Garcia as one of five gangsters about to get hit by the mob for botching a robbery. Of all the things that were bad about the film, the worst was that Denver was horribly miscast as a film noir location. The city's just too pretty.

The sky is too blue, there are too many flowers and trees, and there are way too many people out enjoying life—jogging, sipping beer at brewery tasting rooms, dining on rooftops, kayaking, skiing, mountain climbing, hanging out in coffee shops, window shopping, museum hopping, and just having fun. With three hundred days of sunshine and a mild, dry climate, Denver is an outdoor city. There are forty-two outdoor cafés on just one mile of the downtown 16th Street Mall.

Trendy neighborhoods are expanding every day with new chef-owned restaurants, distilleries, breweries (there are already more than one hundred craft breweries in the metro area alone), galleries, one-of-kind shops, cafés, bakeries, and the list goes on. Picked in several national studies as the No. 1 city in which millennials want to live, the Mile High City is growing on average by a thousand new residents a week.

And then there are the mountains. Half of Colorado is public land, preserved in an incredible collection of four national parks, eight national monuments, eleven national forests, forty-two state parks, three hundred wildlife areas, and literally thousands of miles of hiking and biking trails.

• •

So here is a book about things to do in Denver when you're very much alive.

We cover the city's wild and wooly Old West history; take you to little-known haunts of the Beat Generation; shop at stores frequented by rock stars; introduce you to tasty area specialties like pork green chile and Rocky Mountain oysters; invite you to the region's most fun events and celebrations; guide you on hikes to mountain lakes and waterfalls; escort you on white-knuckle drives and white water rafting; listen to concerts under the stars; taste some craft beer, whiskey, and local cheese; and tell you about everything you need to do to truly experience Denver and the gorgeous Front Range of the Rocky Mountains.

This is big sky country, and for those not used to the West, the distances can seem daunting at first. The seven counties of metro Denver cover forty-five hundred square miles, making it the size of Connecticut. People in Denver think nothing of driving one hundred or two hundred miles in a day to ski, hike, or just have lunch. So the area covered by the book is large—but so are the views. Stand in the rotunda of the Colorado State Capitol and you can see more than two hundred named mountain peaks—a 125-mile-long panorama of snow-covered mountains.

So welcome to the Mile High City. We hope you enjoy your stay however long it is, and that this book guides you to many adventures.

Irene Rawlings Rich Grant

• •

FOOD AND DRINK

FOOD AND DRINK
OF THE OLD WEST

The Buckhorn Exchange was opened in 1893 by a member of Buffalo Bill's band of scouts and holds Colorado's first-ever liquor license. Over the years, it has hosted cattlemen, silver barons, Indian chiefs, astronauts, and five US presidents. The Buckhorn is notable for its meat-centric cuisine (two- to four-pound steaks, buffalo prime rib) as well as a 575-piece collection of taxidermied animal heads that hang cheek-to-jowl in the high-ceilinged restaurant. Dinner entrées range from $28 to $84.

1000 Osage St., Denver, 303-534-9505
buckhorn.com

Julia Child asked for a second helping of roasted marrow bones (called "prairie butter" back in the 1830s) at The Fort, and you will too. But you might also like to sample other authentic Old West dishes in this adobe restaurant. It's a historic replica of Bent's Old Fort, a trading post along the Santa Fe Trail. Favorites here include Rocky Mountain oysters (don't ask—just eat), smokehouse buffalo ribs, elk chops, and ancho chile-orange duck. Dinner entrées range from $20 to $52.

19192 CO-8, Morrison, 303-697-4771
thefort.com

TIP

If you're taking in a concert at Red Rocks Amphitheatre, stop in at The Fort for dinner. The Fort is located just two miles south of Red Rocks. Ask for the 5:30 Red Rocks special menu, and you'll be out in plenty of time for the concert.

EATING AND DRINKING
IN THE NEW WEST

Many world-class chefs call Colorado home and are remaking the culinary landscape of Denver. Here are just a few. Jennifer Jasinski showcases Mediterranean-influenced cuisine at her original restaurant, **Rioja**. Elise Wiggins' signature restaurant, **Panzano**, features a Northern Italian menu and some of the best bread in Denver. Troy Guard owns five or six Denver restaurants. **Guard & Grace**, a hot steakhouse and drinks lounge, is a local favorite. Frank Bonanno's facebook friends (you can be one too) often get a message on a random Monday night when **Mizuna** and his other restaurants are closed: "I feel like cooking. Who wants to join me?" Tyler Wiard helms the popular **Elway's** (named after the legendary Broncos quarterback). Chicken-fried lobster to start, followed by a 28-oz. Porterhouse. Everyone has dinner at **Kevin Taylor's** before the opera or a bite at his restaurant, **Palettes**, in the Denver Art Museum.

Rioja, 1431 Larimer St., Denver, 303-820-2282. Riojadenver.com

Panzano, 909 17th Street, Denver, 303-296-3525, panzano-denver.com

Guard & Grace, 1801 California, Denver, 303-293-8500, guardandgrace.com

Mizuna, 225 E. 7th Ave., Denver, 303-832-4778, mizunadenver.com

Elway's, 2500 E. 1st Ave., Denver, 303-399-5353, elways.com

Kevin Taylor's at the Opera House, 1345 Champa St., Denver
303-640-1012, ktrg.net

GREEN CHILE:
HOT, SWEET, AND SMOKY

The smoky, peppery smell of roasting green chiles hangs in Denver's autumn air. There are chile sellers (you can buy by the bushel or the baggie) and chile roasters along the roadside and in nearly every parking lot on Federal Boulevard and on Santa Fe Drive. It's a staple on restaurant menus—roasted green chile strips, whole peeled chiles for chile rellenos, and chiles combined with pork to make a green chile sauce used for dipping tostidos or smothering burritos and enchiladas. For a list of chile stands and top green chile restaurants, visit denvergreenchili.com.

TIP

Serious green chile aficionados never miss the annual Chile & Frijoles Festival in Pueblo. Rows of booths offer many chile-tasting opportunities—from chile dogs to jalapeño jam. The event's signature dish is a hot, gooey quesadilla.

pueblochilefestival.com

SEAFOOD
WHEN THE OCEANS ARE
TWO THOUSAND MILES AWAY

Yes, good seafood does exist in Denver and tastes as fresh as on any of the coasts. Shipments are flown in seven days a week. The Oceanaire Seafood Room and Ocean Prime are both white tablecloth chains with menus that change daily, depending on what's in season—maybe Alaska's Copper River king salmon or Wellfleet oysters from Massachusetts.

Sushi Sasa offers a sophisticated take on sushi but also serves up delicate tempura and Scottish salmon sashimi. Sushi Den flies its fish in from Japan every day. Check the website for the catch of the day. Jax Fish House has several locations in Denver, Boulder, and Fort Collins. Locals come here for the laid-back atmosphere and the mile-long raw bar. During happy hour, freshly shucked oysters are $1.25. Also try the peel-and-eat shrimp bowl and the lobster BLT.

Oceanaire
1400 Arapahoe St., Denver, 303-991-2277
theoceanaire.com

Ocean Prime
1465 Larimer St., Denver, 303-825-3663
oceanprime.com

Sushi Sasa
2401 15th St., Denver, 303-433-7272
sushisasa.com

Sushi Den
1487 S Pearl St., 303-777-0826
sushiden.net

Jax Fish House
1539 17th St., 303-292-5767
jaxfishhouse.com

HOT NEW NEIGHBORHOOD EATERIES
IN HOT NEW (AND OLD) NEIGHBORHOODS

RiNo (River North) is a newly chic neighborhood where old warehouses and industrial spaces are being turned into lofts, galleries, and restaurants. Check out Acorn (jeans-clad servers, graffiti-covered walls, and perfectly roasted chicken), Comida (tapas), and Meadowlark Kitchen (comfort food and craft cocktails).

LoHi (just across the pedestrian bridge from downtown), once an old Italian neighborhood, has been reclaimed by young professionals and growing families. Yoga studios and trendy restaurants have followed—Linger (rooftop dinners, sunset views, and fish tacos), Old Major (seafood, swine, and wine), LoHi Steak Bar (braised short ribs, chilled oysters, filet mignon), and Gallop Café (classic ham-and-egg breakfasts, big bowls of latte, and a huge Café Cubano for lunch).

Acorn, 3350 Brighton Blvd., 720-542-3721, denveracorn.com

Comida, 3350 Brighton Blvd., 303-296-2747, eatcomida.com

Meadowlark Kitchen, 2705 Larimer St., 303-953-1815
meadowlarkkitchen.com

Old Major, 3316 Tejon, 720-420-0622, oldmajordenver.com

LoHi Steak Bar, 3200 Tejon, 303-927-6334, lohisteakbar.com

Gallop Café, 2401 W 32nd Ave., 303-455-5650, gallopcafe.com

TIP

Stop into Williams & Graham bookstore for a surprise. Behind one of the walls of books, there's a Prohibition-era-inspired speakeasy that *Esquire Magazine* called the "Best Bar in America."

Williams & Graham
3160 Tejon, Denver, 303-997-8886
williamsandgraham.com

Also check out eateries in the South Pearl, Highlands, Old South Gaylord, and Tennyson Street neighborhoods.

South Pearl, 1200-1900 blocks S Pearl, Denver
southpearlstreet.com

Highlands Square, Speer to Perry on 32nd Ave., Denver
highlands-square.com

Old South Gaylord, 1000 block of S Gaylord, Denver
southgaylordstreet.com

Tennyson Street
Between 38th and 46th Aves.
tennysonst.com

SOURDOUGH AND SWEET CAKES
STRAIGHT FROM THE OVEN

Who doesn't love fresh muffins, flaky pastries, yummy cookies, and fresh-from-the-oven bread?

Go to the **Denver Bread Company** for a boule, a sourdough baguette, brioche, and scones. Plus bourbon ginger cookies and chocolate chip cookies (awarded the best cookie in America by *Food & Wine* magazine). **Babette's Bakery** serves crusty French bread and buttery croissants. Visit **Rheinlander Bakery** for German strudels and traditional Black Forest tort. A line extends out the door for New Orleans–style king cakes during Mardi Gras.

Go to **Happy Cakes** for cupcakes (try the slightly spicy Mexican chocolate) and pastel-colored French macaroons. Locals shop here on Tuesdays when the baked goods are half price. Shops are located in Highlands, Longmont, and on Concourse C at Denver International Airport. **Katherine's French Bakery** offers European pastries (like you'd get at a café on Paris's Left Bank). You can order cream puffs, long johns, and cookies shaped like zoo animals, airplanes, and even the Eiffel Tower. **Gateaux** makes custom cakes shaped like butterflies or elephants or fire trucks. Or choose jewel-like petit fours and iced shortbread cookies. During the holidays, elaborate gingerbread houses.

Denver Bread Company
3200 Irving St., Denver, 303-455-7194
thedenverbreadcompany.com

Babette's Bakery
3350 Brighton Blvd., Denver, 303-993-8602
babettesbakery.com

Rheinlander Bakery
5721 Olde Wadsworth Blvd., Arvada, 303-467-1810
rheinlanderbakery.com

Happy Cakes
3434 W 32nd Ave., Denver, 303-477-3556
happycakesdenver.com

Katherine's French Bakery
728 S University Blvd., Denver, 303-282-5888
katherines.org

Gateaux Bakery
1160 N Speer Blvd., Denver, 303-376-0070
gateauxpastries.com

HIGH TEA
AT THE BROWN PALACE

A traditional British high tea in the atrium lobby of the historic Brown Palace Hotel—a tradition in Denver for decades—offers plates laden with cakes, cookies, and cucumber sandwiches. Soft harp or piano music plays in the background. Choose from a long list of teas and coffees . . . or maybe a glass of champagne or a kir royale. Grandmas take their granddaughters here before a performance of *The Nutcracker*. Husbands and wives meet here after a busy day at the office. Girlfriends have a civilized bachelorette party here. Everyone dresses up just a little. And to kick off the holiday season, visitors must see the amazing annual Champagne Cascade—a tower of six thousand glasses filled from the top (it takes 122 cases to fill all the glasses).

17th & Tremont St., Denver, 303-297-3111
brownpalace.com

LET'S TALK
ABOUT FOOD FESTIVALS

During summer and early fall, there's a food festival nearly every weekend. Visit colorado.com for a complete listing. Here are a few of our favorites. The Food & Wine Classic is held annually in June in Aspen and headlines world-famous chefs like Masaharu Morimoto, Marcus Samuelsson, and Jacques Pepin, who talk about food trends and demonstrate their new recipes. Two grand tastings daily.

foodandwine.com/classic

Another favorite is the Olathe Sweet Corn Festival, set in a country fair atmosphere with 150 food booths and all the sweet corn you can eat.

olathesweetcornfestival

The Colorado State Fair in Pueblo awards blue ribbons for the best pie, best cake, and best jam. There's a "Cooking with Cookies" (of the Girl Scout variety) competition and, of course, a midway with funnel cakes, corn dogs, and cotton candy.

coloradostatefair.com

The Denver International Wine Festival is a celebration of wine, food, and travel. Winemakers from all over the world pour more than four hundred wines.

denverwinefest.com

DENVER SCREAMS
FOR ICE CREAM YEAR-ROUND

Sweet Action Ice Cream on South Broadway has freshly baked waffle cones and cookies (for the ice cream sandwiches) and ice cream flavors like biscuits-and-jam and Vietnamese coffee.

Little Man in Highlands is a tiny walk-up shaped like a giant retro milk can. Expect flavors like peach cobbler and salted Oreo and huge ice-cream sandwiches. A long line, even in winter, but worth the wait.

Liks in Capitol Hill is a family-owned creamery around since 1976. Their ice creams can include balsamic strawberry, ancho chile, Jack Daniels chocolate chip, and PB&J.

Bonnie Brae Ice Cream is an old-fashioned ice cream parlor under a bright red roof and a red-striped awning, with a massive list of flavors like deep-dish apple pie and malted milk ball.

Sweet Cow has six locations (Denver, Boulder, Louisville . . . and a Moo Mobile). Try their root-beer float (the root beer comes from Wynkoop Brewing Company).

Sweet Action Ice Cream
52 Broadway, Denver, 303-282-4645
sweetactionicecream.com

Little Man
2620 16th St., Denver, 303-455-3811
littlemanicecream.com

Liks
2039 E 13th Ave., Denver, 303-321-2370
liksicecream.com

Bonnie Brae Ice Cream
799 S University Blvd., Denver, 303-777-0808
bonniebraeicecream.com

Sweet Cow
3475 W 32nd Ave., Denver, and other locations
sweetcowicecream.com

AUTHENTIC ETHNIC
FLAVORS ABOUND

Jerusalem Restaurant offers casual dining near the Denver University campus and serves traditional gyros, perfectly fried falafel, and lemony hummus. For sure try the baklava. Open late.

Domo is a Japanese country restaurant, dojo, and a little museum of sake cups. Eat outside in summer. Many fragrant stews (try the nabemono) and rice bowls (try the sashimi donburi) big enough for sharing.

Arada is a restaurant that encourages you to wipe your plate with the *injera* (spongy flat bread), and, believe me, you'll want to sop up every morsel of the garlic-and-ginger-spiced dishes.

Café Brazil serves South American dishes—seafood stews like Cazuela Columbiana (prawns and a spicy broth of coconut milk and tomatoes) and Piexe de Angola (a shrimp-and-fish stew seasoned with Malagueta chiles).

Jerusalem Restaurant, 1890 E Evans, Denver, 303-777-8828
jerusalemrestaurant.com

Domo, 1365 Osage, Denver, 303-595-3666
domorestaurant.com

Arada, 750 Santa Fe Blvd., Denver, 303-329-3344
aradarestaurant.com

Café Brazil, 4408 Lowell Blvd., Denver, 303-480-1877
cafebrazildenver.com

WHAT MAKES COLORADO LAMB SO YUMMY

Many chefs from New York to San Francisco swear that Colorado lamb is the best in the world. What makes it so good? Yampa Valley sheep live idyllic, peaceful lives in the mountains, where they can nibble on bromegrass, serviceberries, wild carrots, and larkspur, not to mention keep the invasive knapweed under control.

The ultimate way to try lamb? The thirty-six-ounce roasted Colorado lamb shoulder, served family style at the Mercantile Restaurant in Union Station. Chef Alex Seidel knows something about lamb: he owns a sheep farm and Fruition Farms Dairy & Creamery, just twenty minutes south of Denver.

1701 Wynkoop St., Denver, 720-460-3733
mercantiledenver.com

TIP
Cheeses made from sheep's milk are in demand in Denver.
You can purchase Fruition Farm cheeses at
the Mercantile Restaurant & Provisions. Try the sheep's milk ricotta,
Cacio Pecora, or Shepherd's Halo.

VISIT THE MOTHER SHIP OF CHIPOTLE,
THEN TRY OTHER CLASSIC MEXICAN RESTAURANTS

With more than eighteen hundred locations, Chipotle Mexican Grill is one of the largest restaurant chains in the world, serving millions of burritos and tacos every year. And it started here in Denver in 1993. Today, you can still get a signature large "mission style" burrito in a flour tortilla with meat, beans, rice, and fajita veggies at Chipotle's "mother ship," located at 1644 E. Evans.

Other local favorites are El Taco de Mexico (a tiny, family-owned diner that's been dishing out delicious green chile since 1985) and the original Chubby's—no place to sit but you can take your food across the street into Factotum Brewhouse and enjoy your burrito with a fresh beer. Also check out festive El Noa Noa on Santa Fe Drive, upscale Tamayo (in LoDo), and Lola (a Mexican fish house in LoHi).

Chipotle Original
1644 E Evans, Denver, 303-722-4121

TIP
Denver is home to many other "mother ships" that became successful national chains. The first Quiznos at 1st and Grant; the first Rock Bottom Brewery at 1001 on the 16th Street Mall; and the first Chop House Brewery at 1735 19th Street in LoDo.

El Taco de Mexico
714 Santa Fe, Denver, 303-623-3926
eltacodemexicodenver.com

The Original Chubby's
1231 W 38th Ave., Denver, 303-455-9311

Factotum Brewhouse
3845 Lipan, Denver, 720-441-4735
factotumbrewhouse.com

El Noa Noa
722 Santa Fe Dr., Denver, 303-623-9968
denvermexicanrestaurants.net

Tamayo
1400 Larimer St., Denver, 720-946-1433
richardsandoval.com/Tamayo

Lola
1575 Boulder, Denver, 720-570-8686
loladenver.com

HAVE A COCKTAIL
WITH THE GHOSTS OF KEROUAC AND CASSADY

My Brother's Bar, at the corner of Platte Street and 15th Street in LoDo, is the oldest continually operating saloon in Denver, dating back to 1873. It was the favorite watering hole of Beat Generation pals Jack Kerouac and Neal Cassady. Their cross-country adventures were novelized in Kerouac's *On the Road*, much of which takes place in Denver. Now, it's a family-friendly place with a nice outdoor patio, great burgers, year-round Girl Scout cookies, and a killer Italian Swiss sausage sandwich. But the dark, wooden bar area still has an unmistakable late-1940s vibe.

And the atmosphere is more "off the road" than on it. It's possibly the only bar in Denver without a website or even a front door sign.

TIP

Where would Kerouac drink in Denver today? Favorite dive bars (which means they're insanely popular with millennials) are the Candlelight on South Pearl and Don's Mixed Drinks on East 6th Avenue.

Candlelight Tavern, 383 S Pearl, Denver, 720-217-9750
candlelighttavern.com

Don's Mixed Drinks, 723 E 6th Ave., Denver, 303-831-0218
donsclubtavern.com

DINE
IN LARIMER SQUARE'S
TWENTY-PLUS RESTAURANTS

The 1400 block of Larimer was Denver's first block. Here's the story: In 1858, General William H. Larimer Jr. arrived in Denver, liked what he saw, named the main street after himself, and built Denver's first cabin. Denver's first post office, city hall, and mint were located on this block, as were brothels, speakeasies, and billiard halls. By the 1960s, however, it had become Denver's skid row and was scheduled for demolition. Pioneer preservationist Dana Crawford developed it into Larimer Square, and the city's best restaurants have relocated here. Rioja's chef, Jen Jasinski, who won a James Beard Award for Best Chef Southwest, has restaurants here. So do celebrity restaurateurs Troy Guard (TAG), Frank Bonanno (Osteria Marco), Richard Sandavol (Tamayo), and Ted Turner (Montana Grill), and there's a Capitol Grille and Ocean Prime.

1400 block of Larimer St., Denver, 303-534-2367
larimersquare.com

SIP BEER, PLAY POOL
WHERE CRAFT BREWING IN DENVER GOT ITS START

Denver brews more beer than any city in the world. Colorado calls itself "the Napa Valley of Beer," and no wonder. There are more than 250 craft breweries, brewpubs, and microbreweries in the state and nearly 100 in Denver—more if you count the beer bars. Hoppy or malty, smoky or sour, chocolate- or coffee-infused, there's a brew for every taste. Wynkoop Brewing Company, founded in 1988 by now-governor John Hickenlooper, is the oldest and largest brewpub in the state. Regulars gather on the patio to enjoy views of Denver's historic Union Station, eat upscale tavern cuisine, and sip aromatic, amber-colored Railyard Ale. Another favorite is Patty's Chile Beer, a German-style beer flavored with smoked ancho peppers. Upstairs, you'll find twenty-two pool tables.

1634 18th St., Denver, 303-297-2700
wynkoop.com

TASTE THIRTY-FIVE HUNDRED BEERS
AT THE GREAT AMERICAN BEER FESTIVAL

This is the "Super Bowl and Oscars of Beer" all rolled into one—the largest beer competition and suds tasting event in the world. More than 750 brewers attend, pouring out what has been ranked by *Guinness World Records* as the largest beer tasting in history—some thirty-five hundred different beers.

Admission to the event (tickets are sold online in late September but usually sell out in less than an hour) gets you a free tasting glass and unlimited one-ounce samples of anything you want. Strangely, there are usually people selling tickets outside the festival at their face value (around $80), so in a pinch, just show up. But show up early. Everyone has to be carded, so the line to get in can be very long.

Colorado Convention Center, 14th & Stout, Denver
greatamericanbeerfestival.com

DO A DENVER CRAFT BEER CRAWL

There are many ways to visit Denver's ever-growing craft beer scene—by bike, by bus, or on foot. Here are some of the top craft beer tours, or you can create your own by visiting denverbreweryguide.com and making a list of all those close to each other.

If you're walking, you can go from Breckenridge to Great Divide to Jagged Mountain, with a stop at the legendary Falling Rock Tap House (with more than 145 beers on tap) in LoDo (lower downtown).

By bike, you can visit Farm House at Breckenridge Brewery and Saint Patrick's Brewing Company. Both are on or near the South Platte River Bike Trail in Littleton.

The kitschiest tour is Banjo Billy's, which takes you around downtown breweries in a homemade wood-covered bus—with gigantic steer horns on the hood.

TIP
Drink your way around the world. Hogs Head has cask-conditioned English bitter; Prost has authentic German pilsners and wheats brewed in copper kettles from Germany; and Crooked Stave is the place for true Belgian sours.

BY FOOT

Breckenridge Colorado Craft
2220 Blake St., Denver, 202-297-3644
breckbrewcocraft.com

Great Divide Brewing Company
2201 Arapahoe, Denver, 303-296-9460
greatdivide.com

Jagged Mountain Craft Brewery
1139 20th St., Denver, 720-689-2337
jaggedmountainbrewery.com

Falling Rock Tap House
1919 Blake St., Denver, 303-293-8338
fallingrocktaphouse.com

BY BIKE

Farm House at Breckenridge Brewery
2990 Brewery Lane, Littleton, 303-803-1380
breckbrewfarmhouse.com

Saint Patrick's Brewing Company
2842 W Bowles, Littleton, 720-420-9112
saintpatricksbrewing.com

BY BUS

banjobilly.com

Hogshead Brewery
4460 W 29th Ave., Denver, 303-495-3105
hogsheadbrewery.com

Prost Brewing
2540 19th St., Denver, 303-729-1175
prostbrewing.com

Crooked Stave
3350 Brighton Blvd., Denver, 720-550-8860
crookedstave.com

TOUR COORS

Coors is the world's largest brewery and a perfect place to learn how beer is made. You'll see a room of giant copper kettles and then stop in the packaging room, where millions of cans and bottles whirl by on their way to being filled. After the tour, those over twenty-one can sample three free glasses of beer. Try the Colorado Native, a beer only available in Colorado and that claims to be the only "all Colorado" beer made with Rocky Mountain water, Colorado-grown hops and barley, and the oldest strain of brewer's yeast in Colorado. If beer tours bore you, ask for the "short tour," which takes you straight to the free tasting room.

Coors Brewery, Ford St., Golden, 303-277-2337
coors.com

TIP
After touring the world's largest brewery, walk down the street to one of the smallest, Golden City Brewery. The brewery is in the owner's house. Order a beer through the Dutch door of the carriage house, find a table, and relax in the brewer's backyard beer garden.

Golden City Brewery
920 12th St., Golden, 303-279-8092
gcbrewery.com

WATCH A SUNSET
FROM A ROOFTOP BAR

Denver's three hundred days of sunshine a year mean there are also three hundred sunsets worth catching. The best place is the Rooftop bar in Coors Field—the largest outdoor bar at any sports stadium in the nation—that features two decks with 360-degree views of the city and mountains exactly 5,280 feet above sea level (huge numbers mark the exact spot). The bar is fifty-two feet, eighty inches long with fifty-two beers on tap.

Of course, there's also baseball in the form of the Colorado Rockies. A $14 ticket gives you admission to the Rooftop and a $6 bar credit. You can watch the game from anywhere in the stadium—you just won't have a seat.

Coors Field
2001 Blake St., Denver, 303-ROCKIES
coloradorockies.com

TIP
If the game is distracting you from an amazing sunset, cross the street to the View House Restaurant, one of six rooftop bars in the area with volleyboard courts, cornhole, and decks galore.

View House
1215 Market St., Denver, 720-282-1548
viewhouse.com

JOIN THE BOTTLING CREW
AT STRANAHAN'S

Every three weeks, thirty-two regular folks work a five-hour shift at Stranahan's Colorado Whiskey Distillery. They work side by side with the distillers—corking, labeling, capping, shrinking, tagging, boxing, and serving as whiskey quality control. The pay? A free lunch and a bottle of Stranahan's that they've labeled themselves. Here's how it works: you sign up, a lucky fifty are selected for each bottling, and the first thirty-two to respond are in.

Or just go to the distillery for one of eight free daily tours. The hour-long tour explains how Stranahan's Colorado Whiskey is made and includes a free tasting of Colorado's most precious gold. Reservations are recommended.

Stranahan's
200 S Kalamath St., Denver, 303-296-7440
stranahans.com/tours.php

EAT SOME CHEESE

St. Kilian's Cheese Shop & Market in Highlands is chock-full of cheese and charcuterie and its owner cheerfully invites tastes of hearty Gouda or creamy Morbier. Check the website for evenings of cheese and beer or cider pairing. The Truffle Cheese Shop (a cut-to-order shop) and its sister location the Truffle Table in LoHi offer a rotating menu of local and exotic (think water buffalo's milk) cheese and an all-you-can-eat raclette night on Wednesdays. Mell's Cheese in lower Highlands is not only a cheese shop but also a café and wine bar (local craft beers too) that's open for lunch and dinner.

St. Kilian's Cheese Shop & Market
3211 Lowell Blvd., Denver, 303-477-0374
stkilianscheeseshop.com

The Truffle Cheese Shop
2906 E 6th Ave., Denver, 303-322-7363
denvertruffle.com

Mell's Cheese
3000 Zuni St., Denver, 303-455-9555
mellscheese.com

SHOP
AT A FARMERS' MARKET

People forget that one-third of Colorado is flat, agricultural land. Peaches, wine-producing grapes, Rocky Ford cantaloupes, and Olathe sweet corn are the highlights.

In summer, Denver overflows with farmers' markets offering fresh produce, baked goods, herb-infused salad oils, beef and buffalo jerky, salsas, sausages, and fresh-roasted chiles. Throw in live music, food trucks, and breakfast burritos, and there's no better way to spend a Saturday or Sunday morning.

The granddaddy of them all is the Cherry Creek Farmers Market at Speer and University, Saturday mornings from May through October.

On Sundays, hit the South Pearl Street Farmers Market on the 1200 to 1900 blocks of South Pearl, with easy light rail access at the Louisiana St. station, May-November.

Cherry Creek Farmers Market
1st Ave. & University Blvd., Denver, 303-442-1837
coloradofreshmarkets.com/markets

South Pearl Street Farmers Market
1200–1900 South Pearl, Denver
southpearlstreet.com

TIP

In October, visit the pumpkin patches at Rock Creek Farm in Broomfield, just east of Boulder. Go into the fields and gather your own pumpkin, pet ponies and goats, and find your way through six miles of corn mazes.

Rock Creek Farm
2005 S 112th St., Broomfield
303-465-9565
rockcreekfarm.com

Union Station (Scott Dressel-Martin for VISIT DENVER)

MUSIC AND ENTERTAINMENT

GET JAZZED
AT THE PEC

Since the repeal of Prohibition in 1933, El Chapultepec (called "the Pec" by locals) has been dishing out hot Mexican food, cold beer, and even cooler jazz. It's a hole-in-the-wall that hasn't changed much since Prohibition. There's a restaurant and pool table in back, a small bar lined with stools, some booths, and a tiny stage that has welcomed many of the giants of jazz. All three Marsalis brothers, Woody Herman, the entire Count Basie Orchestra, Manhattan Transfer, Artie Shaw, and hundreds of others have squeezed into this tiny club. Don't expect a seat unless you come early. Pop in, squeeze through the crowd for a beer, and enjoy the sounds with an eclectic audience of hipsters, hippies, jazz buffs, millennials, oldsters, and sports fans (Coors Field is just down the street).

1962 Market St., Denver, 303-295-9126
thepeclodo.com

TIP
Stop by Dazzle for retro highballs, small plates, and music in an intimate club atmosphere. Sunday brunch—a great place to wind down a weekend—offers breakfast buffet standards accompanied by jazz standards. Reservations recommended.

930 Lincoln, Denver, 303-839-5100
dazzlejazz.com

DANCE
ON THE RED ROCKS

During the day, this Denver Mountain Park is popular for hiking trails bordered by ancient sandstone formations. At night, it's all about the music. Everyone from the Beatles to Skrillex has performed in this acoustically perfect, ninety-five-hundred-seat natural amphitheater. On a clear night, watch a huge moon rise over the stage with the lights of Denver in the background. It was the film site for U2's classic video "Under a Blood Red Sky" and was picked by *Rolling Stone* magazine as the best outdoor concert venue in North America.

18300 W Alameda Parkway, Morrison, 720-865-2494
redrocksonline.com

TIP
Get a group of ten friends together and book a private backstage tour, which takes you into the Green Room—which at Red Rocks is a "red room" because it is literally carved out of the rock. It's one of the most famous rooms in rock 'n' roll.

Call for reservations: 303-697-6910

GO TO A CONCERT
ON COOL-FAX

Playboy magazine once described Colfax Avenue as "the longest, wickedest street in America." Today, it's just the longest; twenty-six miles of fast food, motels, car dealerships, restaurants, bars and—here and there—some pretty amazing things. Colfax, called "Cool-Fax" by locals, boasts three historic rock emporiums. The Fillmore has hosted Paul Simon, Widespread Panic, Marilyn Manson, and Five Iron Frenzy's final performance. The Ogden Theatre opened in 1919 and hosted such luminaries as Harry Houdini and Sir Arthur Conan Doyle. It switched to movies, then found its niche as a seventeen-hundred-seat rock emporium that presents 125 concerts a year, from Smashing Pumpkins to Nick Cave. The Bluebird opened in 1913 as a vaudeville theater. Seating only 550, it hosts two hundred concerts a year. This is a great place to catch local groups and was one of the starting venues of Denver's own, the Fray.

Fillmore Auditorium
1510 Clarkson St., Denver, 303-837-0360
fillmoreauditorium.org

Ogden Theatre
935 E Colfax, Denver, 1-888-929-7849
ogdentheatre.com

Bluebird Theatre
3317 E Colfax, Denver, 303-377-1666
bluebirdtheater.net

HAVE A SOPAPILLA
AT CASA BONITA

How many restaurants have been featured on *South Park*? This one has.

The moment you walk through the arches of the eighty-five-foot-tall, faded-pink clock tower, you know you are in another world. This thousand-seat, fifty-five-thousand-square-foot theme restaurant has entertained millions since it opened in 1974. See strolling mariachi bands, cliff divers plunging thirty feet into a pool, passageways through volcanos and into old mines, gunfights, gorillas, and pirates.

You slide your tray along a cafeteria line, warmed and illuminated by heat lamps. Folks don't come here for the food. At the end of the meal, a basket of warm sopapillas is brought to your table for dessert. And they are always good.

Part Disney, but mostly its own crazy invention, your kids will love it. After a few margaritas, you will too.

6715 W Colfax, Denver, 303-232-5115
casabonitadenver.com

TRY ON A GENUINE BRONCOS HELMET
AT THE COLORADO SPORTS HALL OF FAME

At this free museum located in Sports Authority Field at Mile High, kids (and adults) can try on official uniforms from the Broncos, Rockies, Avalanche, and Nuggets. See exhibits on the evolution of professional sports, mementos from Sports Hall of Fame winners John Elway and Shannon Sharp and a section about Colorado's women athletes. For a fee (adults $20/children $15), you can take a seventy-five-minute behind-the-scenes tour of the stadium that lets you stand on the field, go in the press box, stop in the visitors dressing room, and see some of the private boxes. Definitely worthwhile for the photos.

1701 Mile High Stadium Circle, Denver, 720-258-3888
coloradosports.org

1000 Chopper Circle, Denver, 303-405-8556
pepsicenter.com/fan-guide/guest-info/tours

TIP
Tour the Pepsi Center, which is as much about the greenroom where Taylor Swift hangs out before concerts as it is for the Nuggets and Avalanche.

SWIM WITH THE SEA TURTLES, DIVE WITH THE SHARKS

An aquarium in landlocked Denver? Yes. The Downtown Aquarium has a million gallons of underwater exhibits containing five hundred species of sea life, but why look at them through glass when you can jump in the water with them? The aquarium offers two in-water experiences. Scuba & Snorkel Adventures don't require certification and let you snorkel and swim with the fishes, including giant groupers, moray eels, green sea turtles, and more. If you're PADI certified, you can dive in the Sunken Shipwreck exhibit with a ten-foot sand tiger shark, sandbar sharks, zebra sharks, and a twelve-foot sawfish. Your friends can stand outside in the viewing area and take photos. Oh, and there are mermaids.

700 Water St., Denver, 303-561-4450
aquariumrestaurants.com

TIP
The aquarium's Dive Lounge has a terrific happy hour from 3 to 7 p.m. weekdays with seats overlooking the giant fish tank. Parking is an expensive hassle, but the aquarium is directly on the South Platte River Bike Trail.

SPEND AN EVENING
WITH LANNIE GARRETT

Lannie Garrett, a brilliant chanteuse and brilliant redhead, opened Lannie's Clocktower Cabaret in the basement of the historic D&F Tower in 2006. For the past decade, the intimate theater has offered an eclectic and enthusiastic assortment of entertainment—from a glamorous Lannie singing Sinatra with a ten-piece swing band backing her up to her country music spoof, "The Patsy DeCline Show." She sings Patsy Cline's greatest hits—"Walkin' after Midnight" and "I Fall to Pieces"—with a unique twist. In between, there are old-fashioned burlesque shows hosted by "Naughty Pierre," comedy, magic, and more music. The cabaret has been called the "coolest room in Denver." It's definitely retro and fun, with chandeliers made of cowboy boots and turquoise beads—you get the idea.

1601 Arapahoe St., Denver, 303-293-0075
lannies.com

TIP
Hailed as one of the top five comedy clubs in the nation, the Comedy Works is another Denver institution. This basement club in Larimer Square has hosted hundreds of national comedians. It's where Roseanne got her start. With its exposed brick walls and cellar-like feel, this is a comedy club from central casting.

1226 15th St., Denver, 303-595-3637
comedyworks.com

DANCE TO A MARIACHI BAND
AT CINCO DE MAYO

Start off with the lowrider parade, graduate to watching Aztec dancers, and finish off munching on street tacos and ears of hot buttered corn in Civic Center Park at the nation's largest Cinco de Mayo celebration. Why Denver? Colorado has more than one million Hispanics (21 percent of the state and 34 percent of Denver residents are Hispanic). Cinco de Mayo honors an obscure 1862 battle in Mexico against the French, and the holiday is hardly even celebrated in Mexico. But in Denver, it has become a celebration of Hispanic culture packed with mariachis, taco stands, lowriders, green chile, folklorico ballet, hip-hop Latino singers, Brazilian dancing, cervezas, and of course, margaritas for all. The event is staged in Civic Center Park the weekend closest to May 5. Top rock groups from Mexico perform on three stages.

Colfax and Broadway, Denver, 303-534-8342
cincodemayodenver.com

TIP
It's always Cinco de Mayo at La Fiesta, the Curtis Park restaurant that has been owned and operated by Michael Herrera since 1964, serving Colorado-Mexican fare. Order the award-winning green chile and chile rellenos.

2340 Champa, Denver, 303-292-2800
lafiestadenver.com

SEE
COLORADO'S LARGEST
HOLIDAY LIGHTING DISPLAY

According to Denver legend, it was Christmas Eve 1914 and young David Jonathan Sturgeon was too sick to come downstairs to see the family tree. To make the night a little brighter for his sick grandson, Denver pioneer electrician D. D. Sturgeon dipped some clear light bulbs in green and red paint and strung them on an evergreen tree in the front yard.

The effect pleased not only the boy, but people came from miles around to see the brilliant, glowing tree. Years later, when Denver decided to decorate the City & County Building, D. D. Sturgeon was hired as a consultant. Today, the City & County Building lighting display is considered to be the largest holiday spectacle in Colorado, with thousands of LED lights. Downtown hotels offer special deals.

The display begins the Friday after Thanksgiving and runs through the end of the National Western Stock Show, the third week of January.

City & County Building
14th and Bannock St., Denver
denver.org/Mile-High-Holidays

TIP
See more than a million lights on the 16th Street Mall and the colorful holiday lighting of Union Station. And don't miss the Parade of Lights—floats and bands march through downtown the first Friday and Saturday evenings in December. denverparadeoflights.com

SPEND THE SUMMER
IN CIVIC CENTER PARK

The only national historic landmark in Denver, this flower- and statue-filled downtown park at the main cross streets of Denver—Colfax and Broadway—hosts some of the city's largest summer events.

The People's Fair, a hippie holdover from the 1970s, is held the first weekend of June. This huge neighborhood party of two hundred thousand people fills the park with music, beer, and dozens of booths celebrating arts, crafts, and local causes.

chundenver.org/peoplesfair

PrideFest brings three 350,000 people, 20 food booths and 250 exhibitors for the biggest celebration of the GLBT community in the Rocky Mountains.

glbtcolorado.org/pridefest/

Stop in the park at lunchtime on Tuesdays and Thursdays from May through October when Civic Center Eats becomes Metro Denver's largest food truck roundup. More than forty trucks and carts offer everything from lobster rolls to empanadas to cupcakes. There are tables and chairs for lunching in and among the flower gardens.

civiccenterconservancy.org

On Labor Day weekend, seek out Taste of Colorado (small bites from Denver's top restaurants) and the Festival of Mountain and Plain (carnival rides, free concerts, and state-fair-type booths selling everything from T-shirts to beef jerky).

atasteofcolorado.com

THROW ON A COSTUME
AND RIDE WITH THE CRUISERS

On Wednesday evenings during the summer, put on a costume, hop on a cruiser, and pedal from pub to pub on the weekly Denver Cruiser Ride. What started in 2005 with thirteen bike-riding friends has become the largest bike cruiser event in the nation. Thousands of riders participate. There are five start locations, but the exact routes are kept secret until the day of the ride. Sometimes the routes end at Civic Center Park with the notorious "Circle of Death"—concentric circles of cyclists pedaling in opposite directions. Not as dangerous as it sounds, but many opt to watch instead of participating.

About the costumes: there's a weekly theme. Previous themes have included bubble wrap, duct tape, and cardboard; pirates, sea men, and mermaids; and ski bums and ski bunnies.

denvercruiserride.com

READ AN OPERA
AT THE DPAC

You don't have to understand Italian to enjoy opera at the Ellie Caulkins Opera House. Just follow along on the seat-back translations. "The Ellie" is a cornerstone of the Denver Performing Arts Complex (DPAC)—the largest in the world under one roof (twelve acres and ten performance spaces). It's home to the Denver Center Theatre Company, the Colorado Ballet, the Colorado Symphony Orchestra, and Opera Colorado. Also wildly popular are Broadway productions. Denver hosted the premiere touring production of *The Book of Mormon* by locals Matt Stone and Trey Parker (the creators of *South Park* graduated from nearby Evergreen High School).

14th and Champa St., Denver, 720-865-4220
artscomplex.com

TIP
Take a backstage tour on Mondays and Saturdays at 10 a.m. Walk-ups are welcome for a ninety-minute tour that goes backstage; into the dressing rooms, costume shops, and design studios; and out on stage. Meet in DPAC's Helen Bonfils Theatre lobby, 14th and Champa, denvercenter.org/events/backstage-tours

TAKE A TRAIN
FROM UNION STATION

Visit the recently restored 1914 Beaux Arts Union Station. The old waiting room has become Denver's hip new living room. You can order a beer through the old ticket windows at the Terminal Bar, snack on oysters and clams at the seafood classic Stoic & Genuine, relax in the pub atmosphere of the Kitchen, or dine on real "farm to fork" dishes at Mercantile Dining & Provision.

Union Station
17th and Wynkoop St., Denver
unionstationindenver.com

Terminal Bar
terminalbardenver.com

Stoic & Genuine
stoicandgenuine.com

The Kitchen
thekitchen.com/next-door-union-station

Mercantile Dining & Provision
mercantiledenver.com

Or . . . board the California Zephyr, just as travelers have done for more than one hundred years. You can clickity-clack all the way to San Francisco or just ride five plus hours to Glenwood Hot Springs, where you can spend the weekend rafting the Colorado River, biking Glenwood Canyon, or floating in the world's largest hot springs pool, then catch the Zephyr back to Denver, admiring a sunset from the observation car.

amtrak.com/californiazephyr

GET YOUR FOLK ON
AT SWALLOW HILL AND THE DENVER FOLKLORE CENTER

Swallow Hill has been kickin' and pickin' in Denver since 1979. Concerts are offered throughout the year—mostly traditional, folk, Celtic, and acoustical music. Also popular are music classes, hootenannies, and sing- and strum-alongs. During the summer there are music festivals (many combined with craft beer) like the annual BrewGrass and Brews & Blues festivals on South Pearl.

Swallow Hill Music
71 E Yale Ave., Denver, 303-777-1003
swallowhillmusic.org

Denver's folk roots go back to 1962, when local legend Harry Tuff opened the Denver Folklore Center. Whether you're shopping for a guitar, need strings for a ukulele, or just want to talk folk music, stop by and visit with Harry. Bob Dylan, Judy Collins, Joan Baez, Pete Seeger, and Doc Watson have all shopped here.

Denver Folklore Center
1893 S Pearl St., Denver, 303-777-4786
denverfolklore.com

TIP

Bring your instrument to the Folklore Center on Monday nights when there's a strum-along open to all who show up.

THREE "MUST-SEE"
PLACES TO WATCH A MOVIE

From small art houses to multiscreen cineplexes, Denver is a great place to see movies. Here are a few of the most unique venues.

The Denver Film Festival is held the first two weeks of November. Cinephiles enjoy more than 250 films from forty countries lighting up screens all over Denver. Dozens of world-famous film directors, actors, editors, and writers attend screenings, introducing their pictures and answering questions from the audience.

Film on the Rocks shows classic films on a giant screen under the stars with the lights of Denver on the horizon and a big moon hanging in the sky. Ride out to Red Rocks Amphitheatre on the Denver Film Society's party bus, which includes round-trip transportation, appetizers, and a cash bar.

Built in 1930, the Mayan Theatre is one of only three art deco Mayan Revival–style movie theaters that remain in the US. This gorgeous theater has been restored and has three screens that show the best in art and indie films. The upstairs lobby has a full bar.

Sie Film Center, 2510 E Colfax, Denver, 270-381-0813
denverfilmfestival.org

Red Rocks Amphitheatre, 18300 W Alameda Parkway, Morrison
720-865-2494, redrocksonline.com, denverfilm.org

Mayan Theatre, 110 Broadway, Denver, 303-744-6799
landmarktheatres.com/denver

GET YOUR GROOVE ON
AT A DANCE CLUB

The club scene in Denver is hot and varied. Expect everything from '60s disco to swing, from salsa to electronica.

Chloe is a chic disco but also a quite good Middle Eastern restaurant. The Euro vibe attracts a young, stylish set. **Bar Standard**, a hot underground electronic music scene, features some of the top spinners in electro and techno music. Oh, and there's Latin music and a rooftop deck with great views.

Vinyl has to be Denver's biggest club, with three floors, each featuring different music (electronica, hip-hop, R&B, and Top 40) and a posh hangout lounge. At **The Church**, don't let the stained-glass windows and beeswax candles in this 1889 church fool you. This place has a booming sound system and is a favorite with locals. Come early. It gets packed. **La Rumba** is the place to go for live Latin music, salsa, rumba, and merengue.

Chloe, 1445 Market St., Denver, 720-383-8447, lotusclubs.com/chloe

Bar Standard, 1037 Broadway, Denver, 720-416-6209
coclubs.com/bar-standard

Vinyl, 1082 Broadway, Denver, 303-506-8078, coclubs.com/club-vinyl

The Church, 1160 Lincoln St., Denver, 303-832-3528
coclubs.com/the-church

La Rumba, 99 W 9th Ave., Denver, 303-572-8006

SPORTS AND RECREATION

DO THE STAIRS
AT RED ROCKS

Sure, it's a world-renowned concert venue, but Red Rocks Amphitheatre is also one of the top places to work out in Colorado. There are 138 steps from the stage to the upper concession area and more than a hundred more steps descending to the lower parking lot. Racing or even just walking the stairs at sixty-four hundred feet above sea level is a true workout. Bring water. People also run the full length of all sixty-nine rows of bleachers (the equivalent of three miles). Denver firefighters train here, doing all of the above while carrying someone on their back. On summer weekends, as many as two thousand people gather at 7 a.m. to find their Zen, do the downward dog, and greet the sunrise with yoga on the rocks. Tickets are $12 and sell out fast.

Red Rocks Amphitheatre
18300 W Alameda Parkway, Morrison, 720-865-2494
redrocksonline.com

BAG A FOURTEENER
THE EASY WAY

Colorado has fifty-four peaks that soar to fourteen thousand feet and higher—more than any other state. Bagging a fourteener is a rite of passage for locals. Here are two easy ways:

Ride Swiss-made cars on the highest cog railroad in the world to the top of Pikes Peak. You can also drive to the 14,114-foot summit. The drive down is so long and steep, there's a station midway that measures the temperature of your brakes. Too hot and you'll have to take a fifteen-minute break to let them cool. Pikes Peak is located ninety miles south of Denver.

You can also drive the highest paved road in North America to the summit of Mount Evans (14,265 feet). The road snakes and curves and there's almost always a herd of Rocky Mountain goats or bighorn sheep to see. It will be twenty-five to thirty degrees colder on top of Mount Evans than in Denver. Bring jackets and expect snow—even in July and August.

Pikes Peak Cog Railway
515 Ruxton Ave., Manitou Springs, 719-685-5401
cograilway.com

Pikes Peak Highway
5069 Pikes Peak Highway, Cascade, 719-385-7325
pikes-peak.com

Mount Evans Highway, Evergreen, 303-567-3000
mountevans.com

CLIMB
LONGS PEAK

Climbing a fourteener is serious business and requires being in good shape and having a lot of determination and lots of luck with the weather. Every year, some fifteen thousand people attempt to summit the 14,255-foot Longs Peak.

For the average person, it's a strenuous, all-day, sixteen-mile climb that requires starting at 4 a.m. or earlier. You always want to be off the summit by noon to avoid lightning. While Longs doesn't require any special mountaineering skills or equipment; many climbers wear helmets to protect against rock falls from above. Carry four quarts of water, as there is no water on the trail.

It's a "long" day, but there are few better feelings in Denver than catching a glimpse of Longs Peak in the distance and knowing you have summited it.

Rocky Mountain National Park, Estes Park, 970-586-1206
http://www.nps.gov/romo/planyourvisit/longspeak.htm

TIP
Easier fourteeners include Grays Peak and Torreys Peak (connected by a saddle), which are the simplest climbs, along with Mount Bierstadt, a relatively short climb from the top of Gunnella Pass. Founded in 1912, the Colorado Mountain Club is a good source for climbing information or climbing partners.

710 10th St., #200, Golden, 303-279-3080, cmc.org

DO SOME RECON
IN ROCKY MOUNTAIN NATIONAL PARK

Rocky Mountain National Park offers more than 400 square miles of preserved natural beauty with 147 lakes, 360 miles of trails, and more than 100 peaks that are 11,000 feet or higher.

Top experiences:

- Drive over Trail Ridge Road (the highest continuous highway in the world) and stop at the visitor center (two miles above sea level). Bring a jacket, hike to the top of the ridge, and throw a snowball—even in summer.
- Pick a backcountry lake (Gem, Bierstadt, Bluebird, Cub, Mills, or the Loch) and hike in for a picnic lunch.
- Catch that big rainbow. There are more than 50 secluded lakes and streams where you can fish. A Colorado fishing license is required.

Rocky Mountain National Park, Estes Park, 970-586-1206
nps.gov/romo

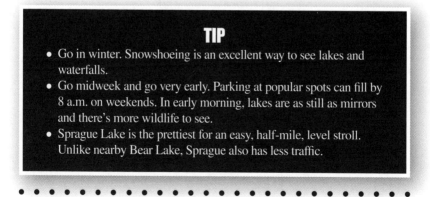

TIP
- Go in winter. Snowshoeing is an excellent way to see lakes and waterfalls.
- Go midweek and go very early. Parking at popular spots can fill by 8 a.m. on weekends. In early morning, lakes are as still as mirrors and there's more wildlife to see.
- Sprague Lake is the prettiest for an easy, half-mile, level stroll. Unlike nearby Bear Lake, Sprague also has less traffic.

EXPLORE
A STATE PARK

The Colorado state parks in the metro area aren't very well known but can be just as spectacular as the national parks.

Roxborough is a completely natural "Red Rocks," without parking lots and roads. Trails wind around and through the seventy-million-year-old rocks. Eldorado Canyon is world famous to hardy bands of extreme rock climbers. For everyone else, it's an easy hike up a spectacular canyon with towering walls above you. Bring a jug and for a small fee you can fill it with fresh water from Eldorado Springs. Staunton State Park is wonderful for mountain biking (seven miles each way) to a waterfall. Golden Gate Canyon has the best mountain panorama on the Front Range. The view stretches from the nearby Indian Peaks to Rocky Mountain National Park and all the way to Wyoming.

All parks: cpw.state.co.us

Roxborough State Park
4751 E Roxborough Dr., Roxborough, 303-973-3959

Eldorado Canyon State Park
9 Kneale Rd., Eldorado Springs, 303-494-3943

Staunton State Park
12102 S Elk Creek Rd., Pine, 303-816-0912

Golden Gate Canyon State Park
92 Crawford Gulch Rd., Golden, 303-582-3707

B-CYCLE
ON 850 MILES OF PAVED BIKE TRAILS

Denver has the nation's first bike-sharing program, B-cycle, which has more than seven hundred bikes available for sharing at eighty-seven year-round stations in ten neighborhoods. You simply swipe a credit card and set off on a sturdy red Trek bike (with lights, basket, and lock). Half-hour rides are free after your daily $9 rental fee and an hour ride is only $1 more. These are bike "shares," not rentals, so short rides are inexpensive, but longer rides of two, three, or four hours get pricey, and a full-day rental is $109. So ride like the Pony Express—go from station to station, and switch bikes often.

Denver B-cycle, denver.bcycle.com

TIP
A remarkable 850 miles of off-street bike trails make it easy to pedal from museum to park to brewery by bike. The Cherry Creek Bike Trail offers a three-mile creek-side ride from downtown to the three hundred plus shops, galleries, and restaurants in Cherry Creek North. Download a bike map at denvergov.org.

CLIMB LOOKOUT MOUNTAIN
AND MEET THE WORLD'S FIRST SUPERSTAR

Buffalo Bill Cody was the world's first superstar—a nineteenth-century Elvis. Beginning in 1883, his Buffalo Bill's Wild West performed in more than a thousand cities in twelve nations, and Bill employed 640 cowboys, Indians, vaqueros, ropers, trick riders, and sharpshooters.

Bill was visiting his sister in Denver in 1917 when he died, and his funeral on top of Lookout Mountain was (and still is) the largest in Colorado history.

All true Coloradans must make a visit and throw a penny on Bill's grave. The museum is fun, with guns, posters, and outfits from the Wild West show.

Buffalo Bill Museum & Grave
987 Lookout Mountain Rd., Golden, 303-526-0744
buffalobill.org

TIP
The best way to the museum is via the Lariat Loop Trail. It's 4.3 miles of curves and turns up Lookout Mountain, all with incredible views. Begin at the intersection of Hwy. 6 and 19th Street in Golden. lariatloop.org

SEE DOWNTOWN
UPSIDE DOWN

Elitch Gardens Theme & Water Park is America's only downtown theme park, which means that when you're looping and twisting and momentarily upside down on Brain Drain, Mind Eraser, or Sidewinder, you have a unique upside-down view of the skyline. It's really two parks in one—there's a full water theme park with slides, wave pools, and rivers, and a theme park with one of America's top ten wooden roller coasters and the Tower of Doom, where you drop two hundred feet at sixty mph.

Elitch's also does magic shows, fireworks, "dive-in movies" (you watch from the pool), brewfests, and the truly frightful Fright by Night (in October, the entire theme park turns into a haunted house at night, including zombies grabbing your ankles from the dark). It takes days to recover.

2000 Elitch Circle, Denver, 303-575-4386
elitchgardens.com

TIP
The scariest ride in Colorado is the Royal Rush Skycoaster at Royal Gorge. You speed off a cliff at fifty mph to momentarily stop and look straight down twelve hundred feet to the Arkansas River below.

Royal Gorge Bridge
4218 County Rd. 3A, Canon City, 719-275-7507
rgbcc.com

STAND A MILE HIGH

The classic mile-high spot is the fifteenth step on the west side of the state capitol, marked by the carved words "One Mile Above Sea Level" in the stone step. Unfortunately, modern technology has proved that the "real" 5,280-foot marker is the thirteenth step, indicated with a brass plaque. (Most people take a shot of their feet on the capitol's carved step and move on.) But the best Denver photo opportunity is the outdoor deck on the west side of the Denver Museum of Nature & Science, which offers a clear unrestricted view of City Park, the lake, the downtown skyline, and the mountains. You're not exactly a mile high, but if you frame the picture to include the park's 5K gravel running path that circles around Ferril Lake, you can point out a spot that is. The path follows the contour and much of it is exactly a mile high.

Lincoln & Colfax Aves., Denver, 303-866-2604
colorado.gov

TIP
There's a giant "5280" on a beam above the Rooftop bar in Coors Field. The beam is exactly a mile high (and the bar beneath it is fifty-two feet, eighty inches long with fifty-two beer taps).

20th & Blake, Denver, 303-762-5437
colorado.rockies.mlb.com

HIKE, BIKE, OR RUN
THE ENTIRE HIGH LINE CANAL

Built in 1883 to provide irrigation water, the High Line Canal meanders for seventy-one miles across metro Denver, passing through three counties and many towns as it heads from Waterton Canyon to the Rocky Mountain Arsenal in northeast Denver. Almost the entire length is level, tree-lined, and accessible to hikers, bikers, or runners; much of it is even open to horseback riding. In fall, hundreds of cottonwoods along its banks turn a burnished gold.

Some parts of the path are paved, while others are rural. At times it's as wide as a road; in other spots it's a narrow track. A helpful mile-by-mile pocket-sized guide is available at Tattered Cover Bookstore. The canal passes near dozens of restaurants, making it the perfect spot for a stroll, say, after a brunch in Old Town Littleton.

303-893-2444, denverwater.org/Recreation/HighLineCanal

CROSS DEVIL'S GATE BRIDGE

Of all the railroad engineering feats in Colorado, the greatest—and scariest—is the Devil's Gate Bridge in Georgetown. The one-hundred-foot-high narrow trestle allows the railroad to corkscrew around and literally cross over itself, just like a Lionel toy train set. The railroad has been restored, and steam trains send huge plumes of smoke up into the evergreens as they chug their way up the valley to cross the bridge. Stand in the open-air gondola car and you can look straight down to the river one hundred feet below. The railroad connects to Georgetown and Silver Plume, towns on the National Register of Historic Places.

Georgetown is forty-two miles west of Denver on I-70, 1-888-456-6777
georgetownlooprr.com

TIP

For more mining history, stop at the nearby Phoenix Gold Mine. This roadside attraction walks you into a one-hundred-year-old mine shaft with a genuine gold vein to look at, and once you're back outside in the warm Colorado sunshine, they'll teach you the fine art of gold panning. Open May-October.

Exit 239 off I-70, Idaho Springs, 303-567-0422
phoenixgoldmine.com

GO TUBING
ON CLEAR CREEK

Yes, the water is cold (much of it was probably snow just the week before) but there are some wonderful tubing adventures along the Front Range, especially on ninety-degree days in August. The Clear Creek Whitewater Park in Golden is especially inviting because there are a dozen man-made whitewater chutes, some light rapids and drops, but also plenty of places to just float along.

You can tube in May and June, but the water can be pretty cold, requiring wetsuits. The folks at Colorado Water Sport will set you up with tube rentals, advice, and maps to tubing on Clear Creek, St. Vrain River, Boulder Creek, and others.

3600 Arapahoe, Boulder, 720-239-2179
whitewatertubing.com

clearcreekcounty.org

TIP
Idaho Springs (twenty-three miles west of Denver on I-70) has become the adrenaline capital of the Front Range, with more than a dozen companies offering all classes of whitewater rafting on Clear Creek, known for having more rapids per mile than most of the other commercial rivers in Colorado.

LOSE YOUR LUNCH, YOUR MIND,
AND MAYBE YOUR SWIMSUIT

What do you do when you're a thousand miles from the nearest ocean? You build the nation's largest water theme park. Water World has forty-eight water attractions on seventy acres. The names of the rides tell you how you can lose your lunch (and maybe your swimsuit) whirling and twisting and being pulled in different directions by waves, water sprouts, and rivers: Screamin' Mimi takes you on a water roller coaster at thirty mph, Storm is pitch black with lighting and sound effects, and Turbo Racer has eight lanes of racing competition. You can go down a raging Colorado River or a slow-and-peaceful Rio Grande. There are big waves and undercurrents at the 1.1-million-gallon Thunder Bay or smaller ones in Captain Jack's five-hundred-million-gallon pool. The big ride of the park takes you five minutes on a Voyage to the Center of the Earth with sudden drop-offs, dinosaurs, and downward spirals.

8801 Pecos St., Federal Heights, 303-427-7873
waterworldcolorado.com

VISIT
THE MOST POLLUTED SPOT ON EARTH

During World War II, the US Army acquired twenty thousand acres of land just ten minutes from downtown Denver and built a huge chemical weapons plant—the Rocky Mountain Arsenal. The plant manufactured napalm, mustard gas, and chlorine and was one of the few stockpiles for sarin, the deadly nerve gas.

After one of the largest environmental cleanups in history, the site has been reopened as the Rocky Mountain Arsenal National Wildlife Refuge. A buffalo herd was reintroduced to the rolling grasslands, and there are more than 330 species of animals and birds living in the refuge, including bald eagles, hawks, owls, and herds of deer. A nine-mile, self-drive road winds through the park and there are ten miles of trails.

What about all the contamination? The visitor center explains how the contaminants were "capped" with a combination of dirt, rock, felt, and other materials, making the area safe for humans and animals.

6550 Gateway Rd., Commerce City, 303-289-0930
fws.gov/refuge/Rocky_Mountain_Arsenal/

TAKE A GARDEN STROLL
IN WASHINGTON PARK

With three hundred days of sunshine, Denver has long been known for its gardens. Frederick Law Olmsted Jr., the son of the famed designer of New York's Central Park, helped design Washington Park. Two lakes, paddleboats, shade trees, bike trails, tennis courts, and a huge area for volleyball tournaments combine with beautiful gardens. The north garden is a formal affair, with geometric crushed gravel paths winding through two dozen flower beds filled with roses, geraniums, and dozens of other plants. The south garden is a replica of Martha Washington's garden at Mount Vernon. Denver's Croquet Club meets here each week; so does the Washington Park Lawn Bowling Club, and lessons for beginners are free.

There are many entrances to the park, but the prettiest is by Smith Lake and the larger garden at W Exposition Ave. and S Downing St.

Denver Croquet Club
S Franklin St. and E Mississippi Ave., Denver, 720-937-3056
denvercroquetclub.org

Washington Park Lawn Bowling Club
washingtonparklawnbowlingclub.com

TIP
If it's dusk and a Thursday in summer, join locals in the boathouse, where Shukr "Sugar" Basanow has been teaching Denverites how to dance for more than forty years. At the Washington Park Boathouse, W Exposition Ave. and S Downing St.

PLAY HOLE 13
AT ARROWHEAD GOLF COURSE

The signature hole at Arrowhead Golf Course (a Robert Trent Jones Jr.–designed course) is the thirteenth—a 174-yard, par three, downhill shot. The course plays around, through, and over three-hundred-million-year-old sandstone rock monoliths. It's difficult to pick a favorite hole, but hole thirteen has an added attraction—foxes that den to the right of the tee box.

Because the air is thinner at seven thousand feet, you don't have to be a power hitter to hit a four-hundred-yard drive. Golf balls travel 10 percent farther a mile above sea level. The downside is that your ball can also go farther into the rough. Everyone at the Kennedy Golf Course (one of seven public golf courses operated by the city of Denver) pauses to get a shot by the sign at the edge of the rough that says, "Caution: Rattlesnakes." They're not kidding either.

Denver's Evergreen Golf Course is carved into the side of a mountain. This short, par sixty-nine course (just over five thousand yards) is known for its narrow fairways and tricky greens. And you might have to play through a heard of elk.

Arrowhead Golf Club
10850 W Sundown Trail, Littleton, 303-973-9614
arrowheadcolorado.com

Kennedy Golf Course
10500 E Hampden, Denver, 720-865-0720
cityofdenvergolf.com/golf-course/kennedy

Evergreen Golf Course
29614 Upper Bear Creek Rd., Evergreen, 303-674-6351
cityofdenvergolf.com/golf-course/evergreen

• •

MOUNTAIN BIKE, HIKE, OR FLY-FISH
IN WATERTON CANYON

Denver's prettiest, closest, and most accessible bit of mountain scenery is Waterton Canyon, featuring a wide, hard-packed dirt road that follows the South Platte River for 6.5 miles below towering rock cliffs. You are likely to see bighorn sheep bounding up rock cliffs, drinking at the river, or even walking down the road. Give them a wide berth—they are accustomed to people, but you don't want to get butted by those horns. You might also see bears. Give them a wide berth too.

The river is also open to anglers (buy a license online at takemefishing.org). Some sections have been damned, offering quiet pools for wily brown trout to lurk; other parts are wild and free flowing.

Denver Water, 303-893-2444
denverwater.org/Recreation/WatertonCanyon

TIP
Park in the free lot at the entrance, 4.1 miles south of CO-470 on Wadsworth Blvd. Because of the abundant wildlife, neither cars nor dogs are allowed into the canyon.

RIDE THE SKI TRAIN,
SKI WINTER PARK

From 1940 to 2009, the Winter Park Ski Train left Denver's Union Station every weekend at 7:15 a.m. and slid to a stop just one hundred yards from the base of Winter Park's ski slopes—the third-largest ski area in Colorado. It was a sad moment when the train stopped operating in 2009.

Now, Amtrak is running experimental ski trains on the same route and wants to bring the train back in 2016. Riding along on ledges through forests of snow-covered evergreens is a bucket list train ride . . . not to mention enjoying a beer in the observation car after a long day of skiing.

Winter Park Resort is owned by the city of Denver and has 320 inches of annual snowfall and 143 miles of trails.

Winter Park Resort
85 Parsenn Rd., Winter Park, 970-726-1564
winterparkresort.com

TIP
Even if you have to drive, Winter Park is still one of the best resorts from Denver since you avoid the traffic at the Eisenhower Tunnel. Once you get on I-70, there's only one stoplight between Denver and the ski area parking lot.

Colorado Railroad Museum

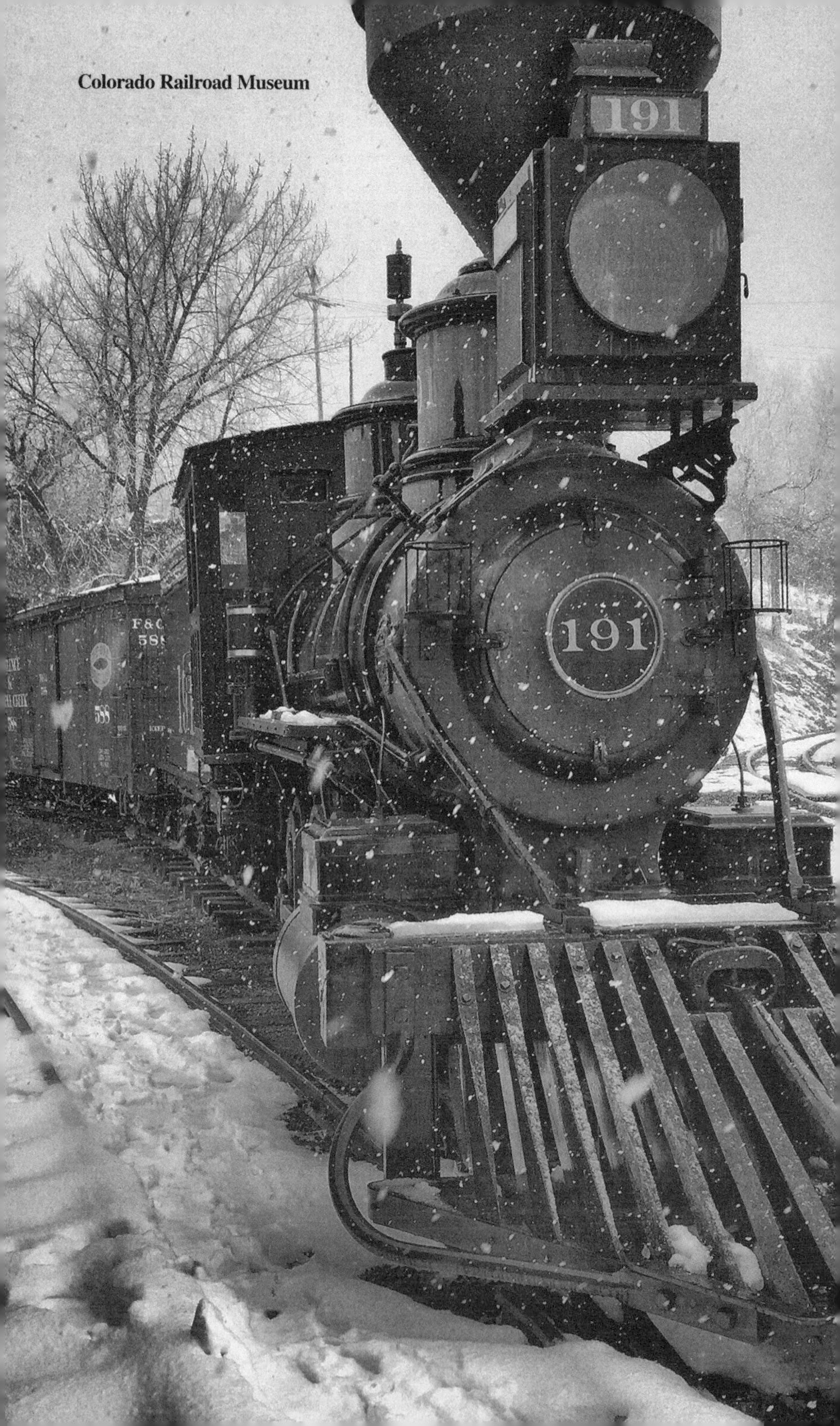

CULTURE AND HISTORY

BUILD A TORNADO
AT NCAR

The National Center for Atmospheric Research (NCAR) is one of the world's top research centers for the study of weather, climate change, and interactions between the earth and the sun. It's also a lot of fun. A free interactive museum is open daily with hands-on exhibits where you can build a tornado, steer a hurricane, play with clouds, and create lightning.

The center is in a spectacular location at the base of the Flatiron rocks (overlooking all of Boulder), and it is housed in one of legendary architect I. M. Pei's masterpieces. Certainly one of his top ten buildings, it looks so futuristic that Woody Allen used it in his science fiction comedy, *Sleeper*.

1850 Table Mesa Dr., Boulder, 303-497-1174
ncar.ucar.edu

TIP
Take the half-mile Weather Trail, stopping along the way to read the dozen plaques explaining why Colorado's weather can be so extreme, different, and, at times, totally crazy.

SEE WHY
ROOM 217 AT THE STANLEY IS THE MOST HAUNTED HOTEL ROOM IN THE US

Stephen King's horror novel *The Shining* has frightened generations of readers. But the book and movie would never have existed if King had not (in 1974) spent a night in room 217 of the Stanley Hotel. At the time of King's visit, the hotel did not have heat and was closing for the winter season. King was the only guest. He dined alone and wandered the empty hotel corridors. That night he had horrible nightmares, but by morning he had the outline of his book about a hotel haunted by its past guests.

Built in 1907, the Stanley has long been known for its paranormal activities. You can learn more on daily ghost tours. Or you can stay in the authentically restored 140-room historic hotel (now open year-round). The most haunted room is 217, but spooky encounters have been reported in nearly every room.

333 Wonderview Ave., Estes Park, 970-577-4000
stanleyhotel.com

SPEND A NIGHT
AT THE BROADMOOR

There's something magical about staying in the Broadmoor's historic (built in 1918) main lodge. Reserve a west-facing room so you see the sunset over the mountains and the early morning sun hitting the lake. Play golf on three courses (the mountain course is most challenging), wind down with wine-therapy treatments at the spa, drink a yard of ale at the Golden Bee (an authentic English pub), or get glammed up and dine at the Penrose Room (Colorado's only five-star restaurant). The Broadmoor is especially magical during the holidays, when lights glow in the trees around the lake and the lodge is filled with live Christmas trees, roaring fires, and a massive gingerbread village.

1 Lake Ave., Colorado Springs, 844-513-9981
broadmoor.com

TIP
For a wilderness experience, stay at the Ranch at Emerald Valley. Ten luxe cabins sit in one hundred thousand acres of national forest, just minutes from the lodge. Or stay ninety-four hundred feet high at Cloud Camp, where twelve cabins and a new lodge have unobstructed 360-degree views of the Rocky Mountains.

SEE A MASTERPIECE
IN A FORMER BORDELLO

The Navarre at 1727 Tremont Place has a checkered past. Opened in 1880, the beautiful brick building with its shiny copper cupola was once a bordello, with a secret tunnel running under the street to the Brown Palace Hotel so guests could visit the young ladies of the Navarre in private.

Today, you can walk in the front door of what is now the American Museum of Western Art and see the private collection of Denver billionaire Philip Anschutz. There are, of course, classic cowboy-and-Indian masterpieces by Frederic Remington and Charlie Russell, but also Hudson River School landscapes (where American Western art began in the early 1800s), illustrations by N. C. Wyeth, and iconic Southwestern paintings by Georgia O'Keeffe. Go online for reservations. Viewing times are limited, as are the number of people who can enter at any one time.

1727 Tremont Pl., Denver, 303-293-2000
anschutzcollection.org

TIP
Attend what locals call "The Art and Cattle Show"—paintings, drawings, bronzes and watercolors (most with a ranch or cowboy theme) sell like hotcakes in the down-home, rodeo-style atmosphere. Annually at the National Western Stock Show.

4655 Humboldt Street (the National Western Complex), Denver
303-297-1166, coorswesternart.com

LEARN HOW TO MAKE MONEY
AT THE US MINT

The first thing you learn on a free tour of the US Mint is that it costs 1.7 cents to make a penny and eight cents to make a nickel. How do they stay in business? They make it up on quarters and half dollars. You'll see coins being made. The Mint produces up to fifty million of them a day. On the tour you see every step of the process—from cutting blanks, to stamping, to bagging and shipping. It's fun seeing the machines spew out new coins like a Vegas slot machine gone mad. The US Mint in Denver is the second-largest storehouse of gold after Fort Knox, so you'll see millions of dollars of gold bars. Make a reservation by going to usmint.gov/mint_tours/?action=startreservation.

320 W Colfax Ave. (tour entrance on Cherokee St.)
Denver, 303-572-9500

DIG A DINOSAUR

The stegosaurus (the Colorado state fossil), allosaurus, and other giants roamed here 150 million years ago in the late Jurassic period. Some of the world's most famous dinosaur fossils were discovered in 1877 in Morrison, Colorado, by a local professor, Arthur Lakes. Their discovery set off a historic dinosaur "gold rush," with scientists from around the world coming to Morrison to search for dino bones.

You can join the search at Dinosaur Ridge, which was declared a national natural landmark by the National Park Service. On the 1.5-mile-long Dinosaur Ridge Trail, you can see—and actually touch—150-million-year-old dinosaur bones that are still imbedded in rock. You can follow dinosaur tracks along a rock face in what has been dubbed "the Dinosaur Highway" and learn why Denver is one of the few places in the world where people have discovered dinosaurs in their backyard.

16831 W Alameda Parkway, Morrison, 303-697-3466
dinoridge.org

LEARN FORGOTTEN HISTORY
AT THE BLACK AMERICAN WEST MUSEUM

Up to a quarter of the cowboys on the great cattle drives of the Old West were African Americans. Many of them were freed slaves who migrated west after the Civil War to take hard, dangerous, and low-paying jobs like herding cattle. Their forgotten story is told at this small museum, the Black American West Museum, built in the one-time home of Dr. Justina Ford (1871–1952), Denver's first black woman doctor. Included in the museum is the Paul Stewart Collection. Stewart was a Denver barber who became fascinated with the idea of black cowboys. He drove around the West, meeting old black cowboys and collecting their oral histories, while rounding up historic photos, hats, saddles, ropes, and other cowboy gear.

3201 California St., Denver, 720-242-7428
blackamericanwestmuseum.org

TIP
Just down the block, the Blair-Caldwell African American Research Library has a seven-thousand-square-foot museum telling the history of African Americans in Denver.

2401 Welton St., Denver, 720-865-2401
history.denverlibrary.org/blair

SEE THE BEST ART COLLECTION
BETWEEN CHICAGO AND THE WEST COAST

The Denver Art Museum has more than sixty-eight thousand works of art and is internationally known for its holdings in American Indian art and its world-class collections of pre-Columbian and Spanish colonial art and artifacts, as well as Western American art. The building—a castle designed in 1971 by Italian architect Gio Ponti and covered with more than a million glass tiles—is silhouetted against the sky like a fort on the Western frontier. The 2006 Daniel Libeskind–designed addition (the Hamilton Building) is an explosive tangle of jutting titanium-clad forms. Somehow it all works. The museum attracts and originates major shows like *Matisse and Friends, Brilliant: Cartier in the 20th Century*, and *Andrew and Jamie Wyeth in the Studio*.

100 W 14th Avenue Parkway, Denver, 720-913-0130
denverartmuseum.org

GET LOST
IN THE DENVER MUSEUM OF
NATURE & SCIENCE

The fourth largest museum in the United States is huge . . . and fun. In its five hundred thousand square feet of space there are more than a million objects ranging from huge dinosaurs to a huge (eight-pound) gold nugget. It also houses one of the world's first digital planetariums and ninety life-sized dioramas of animals from across the globe. There are also Egyptian mummies. Kids can see what it's like to climb a fourteener or land a spacecraft on Mars and are encouraged to "feed" a saber-tooth tiger with their pocket change. The tiger roars appreciatively.

2001 Colorado Blvd., Denver, 303-370-6000
dmns.org

TIP

Spend the night at Night at the Museum.
There are, of course, parties and lectures among
the exhibits, but one of the most fun activities
is the "Camp-In." Children (and their parents or
teachers) spend a night in the museum. They see a
planetarium show and an IMAX movie, explore the
museum's world-renowned exhibition halls, sleep
among the dioramas, and end their adventures
at the Denver Zoo—right next door.

STAND
WITH BIG PAINTINGS
AND GIANT SCULPTURES

Just to the west of the Denver Art Museum, the Clyfford Still Museum houses more than twenty-four hundred works by Still (1904–1980)—about ninety percent of everything he created. Roughly sixty paintings and sixty works on paper by this giant of abstract expressionism are on display at any time in a rectilinear, highly textured concrete building. Never heard of him? Still was an eccentric who disliked selling his works, so not many are on display elsewhere. To raise funds, the museum sold three of his paintings. The price? $114 million.

1250 Bannock St., Denver, 720-354-4880
clyffordstillmuseum.org

TIP

Here's a secret even most locals don't know. Denver Central Library, a few steps away from the museums, has an exceptional Western history department that includes prints by John J. Audubon and Edward S. Curtis as well as paintings by the mighty triumvirate of Western art—Frederic Remington, Charlie (Charles M.) Russell, and Albert Bierstadt. And don't miss the outdoor sculptures—a twenty-one-foot pinto on a huge chair by Donald Lipski and Mark di Suvero's sixteen-ton red sculpture that children love to climb.

10 W 14th Avenue Parkway, Denver, 720-865-1111
denverlibrary.org

DISCOVER A HIDDEN TREASURE:
KIRKLAND MUSEUM OF FINE & DECORATIVE ART

Housed in Vance Kirkland's historic 1910 studio (the oldest commercial art building in Denver), the museum is just a few blocks up 13th Street from the Denver Art Museum. Easily the best thing about this eclectic museum is that the director, Hugh Grant, enjoys guiding interested visitors through rooms full-to-bursting with paintings by Kirkland and other notable Colorado artists, along with excellent examples of twentieth-century furniture and decorative art—Saarinen chairs, Ruba Rhombic glass, complete sets of Russel Wright dinnerware—all displayed in very accessible room settings. In fact, more than thirty-five hundred works are on view at any one time. And the museum features a retrospective of Vance Kirkland's paintings along with six hundred works by other modernist Colorado artists. One visitor paused to note that it was a little like falling down Alice in Wonderland's hole. Alice might have to skip it though; no one under thirteen is admitted.

1311 Pearl St., Denver, 303-832-8576
kirklandmuseum.org

MEET
THE UNSINKABLE MOLLY BROWN

Margaret Brown, a socialite, philanthropist, and activist who was most famous for her heroic role during the sinking of the luxury liner RMS *Titanic* in 1912, lived in a grand red sandstone house at 1340 Pennsylvania Street. The house is open for guided tours and furnished as it was in her day. A lively exhibition schedule can feature, for example, vintage fashions, showing how they reflected social changes in America from the Gilded Age through the Great Depression. The exhibitions include runway shows and workshops like "Making Your Own Millinery Masterpiece." High tea (often with holiday or seasonal themes) is offered on Saturdays. Private candlelight, *Titanic*-themed dinners (an eight-course menu featuring foods and wines reminiscent of the *Titanic* era) can be arranged.

1340 Pennsylvania St., Denver, 303-832-4092
mollybrown.org.

TIP
The Governor's Residence nearby is open for free scheduled tours that are especially popular when the home is decorated for the holidays.

400 E 8th Ave., Denver, 303-837-8350
coloradoshome.org

FLY OFF A SKI JUMP
AT HISTORY COLORADO CENTER

This twenty-first-century museum (opened in 2010) is dedicated to making history fly—literally fly—off the pages of dusty old books. The most popular exhibit simulates a ski jump in Steamboat Springs, where you have to bend, twist, and turn exactly right to "land" the jump. Failures watch themselves tumble in a ball of snow. The "Denver A to Z" exhibit is a fun lesson in the history of the Mile High City. Try on the costume worn by Bronco super-fan "the Barrelman," pose with a miniature model of the Blue Bear, or learn about the bodies once buried under Cheesman Park. There are references and mementos in the exhibit of almost everything in this book, from the Brown Palace to Red Rocks.

1200 Broadway, Denver, 303-447-8679
historycolorado.org

TIP

For more history, visit Four Mile History Park. The twelve-acre park preserves what was once a six-hundred-acre farm and stagecoach stop with historic barns, farm animals, and, in summer, old-fashioned baseball games.

715 S Forest, Denver, 720-865-0800
fourmilepark.org

SMELL A PLANT:
WARNING ... IT MAY BE STINKY

See many thousands of plants and extensive plant collections from alpine and aquatic to native and tropical at the Denver Botanic Gardens located on twenty-three acres in the Cheesman Park neighborhood. A recent and rare blooming of the corpse plant (it smells like, well, a corpse) had lines around the block. Expect big exhibits like the glass sculpture of Dale Chihuly or Deborah Butterfield's minimalist horse sculptures (cast bronze, but painted to look like driftwood) and small ones like antique and contemporary botanic illustrations. Locals line up for the Blossoms of Light (annually from late November) and the eight-acre corn maze (held at the Chatfield location in the fall).

1007 York St., Denver, 720-865-3500
botanicgardens.org

TIP
Take your tots to Mordecai Children's Garden, a magical three-acre oasis on the roof of the York Street parking structure, to hunt for bugs in the Glorious Grasslands and to observe aquatic life at Pipsqueak Pond.

GET KISSED
BY BUTTERFLIES AND TICKLED
BY A TARANTULA

Visit the Butterfly Pavilion—a zoo of small wonders. Yes, it's not a big place, but there are more than twelve hundred butterflies fluttering around the open room and even landing on your shoulders as you walk down gravel paths through an indoor rainforest—their natural habitat. Wear a floral dress or Hawaiian shirt to attract even more butterfly attention. Butterfly hatchings take place behind glass (fascinating to watch) and the newbies are released every day. In another room, find stink bugs, praying mantises, and ladybugs. Stand in line to hold Rosie, a Chilean tarantula. She walks lightly over your palm, tickling you with her hairy legs.

6252 W 104th Ave., Westminster, 303-469-5441
butterflies.org

MEET MOTHERSBAUGH
IN LOWER DOWNTOWN

Even when LoDo (lower downtown—near Union Station) was down on its luck, it encompassed one of the finest collections of late nineteenth-century commercial buildings in the American West. Now, most of the buildings in this twenty-three-square-block warehouse district have been turned into art galleries, antique shops, and restaurants. The Adjaye-designed Museum of Contemporary Art, a non-collecting museum modeled after the European *kunsthalle*, has made its hip home in LoDo. Expect shows by the likes of Mark Mothersbaugh, co-founder of the post-punk band Devo and, later, score composer for many of Wes Anderson's films, but also a closet artist for more than five decades. Many notable galleries are clustered close by.

1485 Delgany St., Denver, 303-298-7554
mcadenver.org

TIP
Don't miss Denver's public art, especially the forty-foot tall Blue Bear at the Colorado Convention Center and the Blue Mustang with the glowing red eyes as you leave Denver International Airport.

DO THE FIRST FRIDAYS ART WALK

Museo de las Americas anchors the art district on Santa Fe Drive in a historically Hispanic neighborhood and showcases artists well known in Mexico and Latin America, but often unknown in the United States. Located near downtown, the Santa Fe Arts District has attracted dozens of Denver's more prestigious galleries. Thousands come to this area's festive First Fridays event when galleries and artists' studios serve wine and are open late.

Museo de las Americas
861 Santa Fe Dr., Denver, 303-571-4401
museo.org

Santa Fe Arts District, between Alameda and 12th Aves.
on Santa Fe Drive and Kalamath St.
artsdistrictonsantafe.com

TIP
First Fridays are popular citywide and include Belmar Block 7, Golden Triangle Museum District, Navajo Street Arts District, Tennyson Street Cultural District, 40 West Art District, and RiNo. Each neighborhood stays open late with gallery showings, live music, art demonstrations, and food trucks.

TIP

The most popular event during Denver Arts Week (held annually in November) is the free Night at the Museums. More than twenty of Denver's museums stay open late (until 10 p.m.), and free shuttles make it easy to explore multiple museums during the evening.

denver.org/denver-arts-week

ALL ABOARD
AT THE COLORADO RAILROAD MUSEUM

At one point, there were two thousand miles of narrow-gauge tracks—burrowing through rock, crossing trestles over rivers, and climbing steep canyons—to connect Denver with mountain mining towns.

The Colorado Railroad Museum in Golden has a half-mile circle that is like a giant's toy train layout. You can ride a live steam train (once a month, check the website for schedules). They also have a rare Galloping Goose—a 1923 Pierce-Arrow limousine mounted on wheels with a bus attached to the back. This have-to-see-it-to-believe-it train now offers a bumpy, noisy, and extremely fun run around the tracks.

At Christmas, the Polar Express steams in three times every night. Santa hops on board and hands every passenger a small silver bell. Cold weather makes the steam clouds rise higher and, in the dark, with the soundtrack of *Polar Express* playing, the whistle blasting, and the bell ringing, it's a cacophonous but magical moment.

17155 W 44th Ave., Golden, 303-279-4591
coloradorailroadmuseum.org

GO BEHIND THE CLOCK FACE
IN THE D&F TOWER

Denver's historic D&F Tower is the most famous and iconic building in downtown. When the tower was built in 1911 as part of the Daniels & Fisher department store, the 393-foot tower (modeled after St. Mark's Basilica in Venice) was the tallest structure west of the Mississippi. The department store was demolished in the 1970s but the tower was saved.

On Saturdays, you can take a forty-five-minute tour that goes behind the huge Seth Thomas clock, climb a spiral staircase up the top of the tower, and go outside on two outdoor decks for panoramic views of downtown and the mountains.

1601 Arapahoe St., Denver, 303-293-0075
clocktowerevents.com

TIP
Thinking of getting engaged? You can rent the tower for just one hour for your proposal. They will help devise a way to keep it secret, and you can bring your own champagne.

WEAR A COWBOY HAT
AT THE NATIONAL WESTERN STOCK SHOW PARADE AND CATTLE DRIVE

The National Western Stock Show & Rodeo turns the Mile High City into the ultimate cowtown for sixteen days in January. More than 640,000 people dust off their Stetsons and ride out to the Stock Show grounds for two weeks of bronco busting, steer roping, and barrel racing fun. Kids love the petting zoo with dozens of small barnyard animals—sheep, chickens, pigs, and rabbits—to pet. Food is a big part. As you would suspect, beef is always on the menu—from hot dogs to enormous steaks—but for a real treat—try the pork chop on a stick.

4655 Humboldt St., Denver, 303-297-1166
nationalwestern.com

TIP

The Stock Show Parade is held on the Thursday before the show begins. The parade leads off with cowboys driving forty Texas longhorn steers down 17th Avenue in downtown Denver. There are horses, stagecoaches, rodeo queens, and a cowboy riding a Brahma bull. You can get your picture taken on the bull after the parade.

17th from Wynkoop St. to Tremont Pl.

SEE ART.
CATCH A PERFORMANCE.
LEARN PHOTOGRAPHY.

The Arvada Center for the Arts & Humanities offers year-round theater, classes and art galleries, a historical museum and a wide variety of classes—from photography and ceramics to ballet and modern dance. Bring a picnic and sit outdoors to enjoy jazz, bluegrass or classical chamber music. Vising musicians can include Charlie Musselwhite, Eddie Palmieri's Latin Jazz Band or Julieta Venegas. Check the summer calendar. During the year, expect art exhibitions by local, regional and nationally acclaimed artists. In December, a much anticipated art market offering an appealing array of art, craft, pottery, silver and metalwork by local artists at affordable prices.

6901 Wadsworth Blvd., Arvada, 720-898-7200
arvadacenter.org

TIP

Don't miss Olde Town Arvada—eight miles northwest of Denver—craft breweries, a slew of restaurants and a collection of trendy, one-of-a-kind shops, all housed in turn-of-the-century brick storefronts.

Olde Town Arvada, 7307 Grandview Ave., Arvada, CO, 303-420-6100
oldetownarvada.org

CHERRY CREEK ARTS FESTIVAL

Every Fourth of July weekend, Cherry Creek North hosts Denver's largest celebration of art—the Cherry Creek Arts Festival. The streets are blocked off, and more than 350,000 people attend to see the works of 260 juried and award-winning artists from across America. You'll see photography, sculpture, oils, prints, jewelry, and pottery. Some is museum quality, and some is by emerging artists, so it's still quite affordable. Visual and performance artists demonstrate on several stages. For kids, there's a supervised art studio where they can make their own masterpieces. Stroll along Culinary Avenue to sample small plates—everything from savory crepes to Italian ices. Local craft brewers and distillers offer samples. See cutting-edge art installations like last year's chandelier harp.

On 2nd and 3rd Aves. between Clayton and Steele Sts.
cherrycreekartsfestival.org

TIP
Parking is difficult. There are free bike corrals, making it easy to pedal to the free event.

SEE
THE THIRTY-GALLON BIG FLUSH

The Children's Museum of Denver reopened in the fall of 2015 with more than double its original exhibit and program space. Kids ages four to ten will thrill to Altitude, the three-and-a-half-story climbing structure with a swaying bridge and a ski-country gondola. Don't worry. There are emergency exit doors on each level for tots who suddenly realize they've ventured too high. The newest exhibits are water based with elaborate whirlpools, pumps, geysers, and the thirty-gallon Big Flush that mimics the action of a toilet. Kids love it.

2121 Children's Museum Dr., Denver, 303-433-7444
mychildsmuseum.org

TIP

Visit Tiny Town, a kid-sized town near
Morrison and about half an hour west
of Denver. Opened to the public in 1920,
it has that vintage charm, with eighty pint-sized
buildings (including a grocery store, hotel, barber shop,
and school) and its own ride-aboard steam train.
Take a picnic lunch.

6249 S Turkey Creek Rd., Morrison, 303-697-6829
tinytownrailroad.com

SOLVE A MURDER
AT CHEROKEE RANCH

The ranch was homesteaded in the late nineteenth century and preserved by a wealthy cattlewoman (she bred Santa Gertrudis cattle here). Her name was Mildred Montague Genevieve Kimball, but everyone called her "Tweet." When she died, she willed her thousands-of-acres ranch to be protected as a wildlife sanctuary. Her home (honestly, it's a Scottish castle) is a museum that shows Tweet's collection of art, furniture, and memorabilia from her travels around the world. You can see views of the entire Front Range from the porch. The Colorado Symphony performs here. So does the Denver Center Theater. You can have a tour and an authentic English-style tea or sign up for one of the much-anticipated Murder Mystery Dinners. Was it the butler in the pantry? Or maybe Colonel Mustard in the billiard room with the candlestick?

6113 N Daniels Park Rd., Sedalia, 303-688-555
cherokeeranch.org

TWIRL
WITH DENVER'S DANCING QUEEN

Acclaimed dancer, choreographer, and artistic director of Cleo Parker Robinson Dance, Ms. Cleo has collaborated with many well-known like her mentor Maya Angelou, and she's danced with Merce Cunningham and Twyla Tharp. Her school has an ongoing curriculum of diverse dance classes for all levels (starting with children from the age of three). You can learn African rhythms, breakdancing, creative dancing, hip-hop, jazz, and ballet. Don't dance? You can just watch. Recently, the company performed *Uncle Jed's Barbershop*, based on a Coretta Scott King Award–winning book by Margaree King Mitchell.

119 Park Ave. W, Denver, 303-295-1759
cleoparkerdance.org.

Rockmount Ranchwear

SHOPPING AND FASHION

WEAR A ROCKMOUNT
SNAP-BUTTON SHIRT

In 1949, Papa Jack Weil invented the modern cowboy shirt by using snaps instead of buttons. The shirts started showing up in Western movies and were loved by everyone from Clark Gable to Elvis. A legend was born.

Papa Jack made and sold Rockmount shirts on Wazee Street until he passed away at age 107. Today, his grandson Steve Weil runs the business in the oldest surviving store in LoDo. Every square inch is packed with Western shirts, hats, belts, buckles, and boots. Bob Dylan, Bruce Springsteen, and Sting have shopped here, and you'll see Rockmount shirts on everyone from Paul McCartney to Eric Clapton. As Papa Jack said, "The West is not a place, it's a state of mind." And that means if you're wearing a Rockmount shirt, you take the West with you wherever you go. Be sure and say hi to Wazee, the store watchdog, who greets all customers.

1629 Wazee St., Denver, 303-629-7777
rockmount.com

GET IN TOUCH
WITH YOUR INNER COWGIRL

If you're addicted to boots, Cry Baby Ranch is the place for you. Cry Baby Ranch has been in business for more than twenty-five years, catering to Denver's urban cowgirls and cowboys and their young buckaroos. Slip on a pair of sleek and simple black boots or maybe a pair inlaid in red and stitched with sparkly gold. The clothing (some by Double D Ranchwear, a family-owned business based in Yokim, Texas) is embroidered, beaded, and embellished with silver studs. Or maybe try a hand-tooled leather belt with a trophy buckle. And who wouldn't want to wrap their newborn in a Pendleton blanket, designed by contemporary Native American artists with proceeds going to the American Indian College Fund?

1421 Larimer St., Denver, 303-623-3979
crybabyranch.com

SPEND A DAY
WITH THOMAS AT CABOOSE HOBBIES

Caboose Hobbies is listed in *Guinness World Records* as the largest model railroad store in the world. There are more than one hundred thousand model locomotives, houses, trees, trestles, cars, little people, and track stacked from floor to ceiling (be sure to look at the ceiling to see the model train that circles the building). The trains come in all sizes, some as small as a thumbnail, others large enough to be driven by chipmunks. Scattered throughout are intricate dioramas with city scenes and hundreds of tiny people. There are train videos and books, and if you get bitten by the model-railroading bug, they offer free seminars on everything from how to build scenery to painting a boxcar. There's even a special kids area where junior engineers can push Thomas up and down wood bridges and tracks.

500 S Broadway, Denver, 303-777-6766
caboosehobbies.com

TIP
If your big and small kids would rather visit Middle Earth,
head to the Wizard's Chest, Denver's largest and most innovative
collection of games, costumes, makeup, masks, role-play and all the
swords, light sabers, daggers and other plastic weapons you'll ever need.

415 Broadway, Denver, 303-321-4304, wizardschest.com

BROWSE
DENVER'S RODEO DRIVE: CHERRY CREEK NORTH

It's a sixteen-square-block area filled with one-of-a-kind boutiques, restaurants, spas, and galleries. Most of the four hundred retail shops here are not chains, but small unique businesses—selling everything from blown-glass bowls to handmade silk underwear to fair-trade handcrafts. The tree-lined streets are decorated with gardens and statues, making it one of the nicest and most exclusive places to browse, window shop, sip, or dine. Coffee shops—Starbucks and local roasts—beckon for a quiet sit-down.

And of course it's directly across the street from the city's number one visitor attraction, the Cherry Creek Shopping Center, which is the premier shopping experience in the Rocky Mountains, with 160 stores including forty exclusives such as Neiman Marcus, Tiffany, Anthropologie, Nordstrom, and Ralph Lauren.

Cherry Creek North
Sixteen-block District between 1st & 3rd Aves., between University and Steele Sts., Denver, 303-394-2904
cherrycreeknorth.com

Cherry Creek Shopping Center
3000 E 1st Ave., Denver, 303-388-3900
shopcherrycreek.com

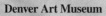
Denver Art Museum

SHOP
THE MASTERPIECES

Museum shops are the best for well-designed, one-of-a-kind gifts—to give that special someone or to keep for yourself.

The Denver Art Museum has large and luscious art books, Bhutanese silk scarves, blown-glass vases, and other stylish objets d'art.

The Kirkland Museum's compact gift shop is stuffed with mid-century pottery and totes emblazoned with Vance Kirkland's signature dot paintings.

At Leanin' Tree Museum and Sculpture Garden of Western Art, choose from more than three thousand posters, greeting cards, and mugs with images from the museum collection.

The Buffalo Bill Memorial Museum offers reproduction posters from Buffalo Bill's Wild West shows, T-shirts with Buffalo Bill's image, and a ton of books about Buffalo Bill and the American West.

Denver Art Museum, 100 W 14th Avenue Parkway, Denver, 720-913-0130
denverartmuseum.org

Kirkland Museum, 1311 Pearl St., Denver, 303-832-8576
kirklandmuseum.org

Leanin' Tree Museum, 6055 Longbow Dr., Boulder, 303-729-3412
leanintreemuseum.com

Buffalo Bill Memorial Museum
987½ Lookout Mountain Rd., Golden, 303-526-0744
buffalobill.org

READ A BOOK.
MEET THE AUTHOR.

With three locations in the Denver metro area, one at Denver International Airport and a new one in Union Station, the Tattered Cover Bookstore is widely regarded as one of the top independent booksellers in the country. Furnished with overstuffed chairs and sink-into sofas, the charming shops offer quiet places to curl up and read—in the company of more than 250,000 books. Each year, Tattered Cover hosts over four hundred readings and literary events. The notable quotables who have come to sign their books include Harry Potter's creator J. K. Rowling, *Twilight's* Stephenie Meyer, Caroline Kennedy, Garrison Keillor, celebrity chef Julia Child, astronaut John Glenn, President Barack Obama, Disney bestseller Rick Riordan, and futurist architect Buckminster Fuller who, even with a broken finger, signed books for a sell-out crowd.

Colfax Avenue, 2526 E Colfax, Denver, 303-322-7727
LoDo, 1628 16th St., Denver, 303-436-1070
Aspen Grove, 7301 South Santa Fe Drive, Littleton, 303-470-7050
Union Station, 1701 Wynkoop Street, Denver, 720-420-5300
tatteredcover.com

HUNT FOR TREASURES
ON ANTIQUE ROW

You'll drive down the street not believing your eyes. There are one-hundred-plus antique shops packed cheek to jowl into eighteen blocks on South Broadway (SoBo). But beyond the antiques, there's an interesting mix of neighborhood taverns serving cold beer and hot sandwiches, vintage and up-and-coming designer clothing stores, ethnic restaurants, and live music venues. Stop at Finders Keepers for a huge selection of Bakelite bangles, Turn of the Century Antiques for an amazing collection of porcelain dolls, All Hours for an excellent stock of antique and vintage watches, and Black Tulip Antiques for a well-curated collection of English pottery, coin silver, tribal carpets, and botanical engravings. And tucked in amidst all of this splendor, you'll discover one of the best Arc Thrift Stores in Denver.

From 1100 to 1800 S Broadway.
Download a map atantique-row.com.

DRESS AND ENTERTAIN
FOR LESS ... MUCH LESS

Visit **Ali's Closet Consignment Boutique** for high-end clothing like Carolina Herrera blouses, Ferragamo shoes, and Nancy Gonzalez bags. Some items worn only once.

Go to **La Cache** (sales benefit Children's Hospital Colorado) for Spode china service for twelve (with all of the serving pieces), Waterford crystal, and monogrammed Irish table linens. Check the Blue Light room for great bargains.

Rags carries Kate Spade and Prada bags, Eileen Fisher cashmere, and Missoni knits. **Plum Consignment** for stylish Coach bags, Diane von Furstenberg wrap dresses, and Neiman Marcus sweaters.

Common Threads in Boulder has higher-end clothing and accessories—Versace, Rebecca Taylor, Bottega Veneta. Half the store is devoted to the art of making clothes (sewing and knitting classes). Check out the Recycled Runway, where teen designers use materials like soda can pop tops, bike tubes, window blinds, and zip ties to make unique outfits. Held annually at the Boulder Theater.

Ali's Closet Consignment Boutique
1610 E Girard Pl., Cherry Hills Village, 303-843-9956
alisclosetconsignment.com

La Cache
400 Downing St., Denver, 303-871-9605
childrenscolorado.org

Rags
201 University Blvd, Denver, 720-508-3181
2027 W 32nd St., Denver, 303-953-0816
3129 28th St. Boulder, 303-440-5758
iloverags.com

Plum Consignment
2373 Central Park Blvd., Denver, 303-322-7586
plumgood.com

Common Threads
1575 S Pearl, Denver, 720-379-4598
2707 Spruce St., Boulder, 303-449-5431
shopcommonthreads.com

CLIMB THE PINNACLE
AT REI

Denver's active outdoor lifestyle has generated more sporting goods stores per capita than any other city. One of the best places to outfit yourself for skiing, hiking, biking, camping, paddling, rock climbing, fitness, and snowboarding is the REI flagship store. Located at the confluence of the Cherry Creek and South Platte River bike trails, the store fills every inch of the gigantic brick 1901 Tramway Building.

But the first thing you see is the forty-seven-foot-high Pinnacle, a hand-sculpted rock monolith that has twelve rope climbing routes and two lead climbing routes ranging in difficulty from 5.4 to 5.13 on the Yosemite Decimal System. The Pinnacle offers everything: hand cracks, finger-cracks, roofs, overhangs, and slabs. There are routes for beginners and experts, and all climbs are free to REI members.

1416 Platte St., Denver, 303-756-3100
rei.com

TIP
After you've summited the Pinnacle, visit the American Mountaineering Museum in Golden—the only museum in the US dedicated to the history of climbing.

710 10th St., Golden, 303-996-2755
mountaineeringmuseum.org

GET YOUR VINYL ON
AT WAX TRAX

Sure, you can get most of your music at iTunes, Amazon, and Pandora. But for the truly obscure, head to Denver's oldest underground record store, Wax Trax. This Capitol Hill fixture has been around since 1975 and specializes in hard-to-find new and used vinyl, CDs, and tapes.

Twist & Shout, the city's largest music store, is located next to the Tattered Cover and across from East High School on Colfax. You can easily spend a day here, listening to any CD you like before purchasing. It's also the place to learn about the local music scene. Located midway between the Ogden and the Bluebird concert halls on Colfax, this is base camp for Denver's growing rock scene, which has already produced the Flobats, the Fray, Fireball, Big Head Todd, One Republic, and the Lumineers.

Wax Trax, 638 E 13th Ave., Denver, 303-860-0127
waxtraxrecords.com

Twist & Shout, 2508 E Colfax, Denver, 303-722-1943
twistandshout.com

Breckenridge

DAY TRIPS

GET YOUR WILD WEST ON
IN CHEYENNE, WYOMING

Cheyenne is only a two-hour drive from Denver, but it's a world away in atmosphere. More than any other single place, Cheyenne was the center of the Old West. Gunslinger Wild Bill Hickok got married here, Wyatt Earp, Doc Holliday, Luke Short, and "Calamity Jane" all called Cheyenne home, and legendary murderer Tom Horn was hanged on Main Street. Every July, four hundred thousand people head to Cheyenne Frontier Days—the largest rip-roaring outdoor rodeo in the world. It's perhaps the only time when even city slickers can walk around in a cowboy hat and boots without feeling self-conscious, because everybody does.

There are many Old West cowboy bars (try the historic 1911 Plains Hotel). But there are also three breweries, including a spectacular one in the old 1887 Union Pacific Depot—the Cheyenne Brewing Company. The depot also has one of most famous and acclaimed model railroad displays in the nation.

The Nelson Museum of the West has outfits worn by Roy Rogers and Dale Evans and historic paintings and artifacts, but everywhere you look in town there are shops selling cattle horns, Western snap-button shirts, 10-gallon hats, belt buckles, and of course, boots made out of everything from ostrich hide to rattlesnake. Yee-haw!

Cheyenne Frontier Days, Cheyenne, 800-227-6336, cfdrodeo.com

The Plains Hotel, 1600 Central Ave., Cheyenne, 307-638-3111
theplainshotel.com

Cheyenne Brewing Company, Union Pacific Depot, Cheyenne
307-514-2525, cheyennebrewingcompany.com

Nelson Museum of the West, 1714 Carey Ave., Cheyenne, 307-635-7670
nelsonmuseum.com

TIP

Seven miles south of Cheyenne, on the Wyoming-Colorado border, stop at the Terry Bison Ranch. A custom-built and very funky private train pulls passengers on standard-gauge tracks across rolling grasslands into the middle of a herd of twenty-five hundred buffalo. You can feed the critters, and there's also horseback riding and a famous buffalo and steak house restaurant.

Terry Bison Ranch
511–25 Service Rd. East, Cheyenne
307-634-4171
terrybisonranch.com

CARRY ON
AT A COLORADO CAMPUS IN BOULDER AND FORT COLLINS

The "Rocky Mountain Showdown" between the University of Colorado and Colorado State University is one of the oldest rivalries in college football, dating back to 1893. But the rivalry between these two schools (and their home base towns of Boulder and Fort Collins) goes much deeper than football. There are debates about which town has the prettier campus, better bike trails, and even better beer.

For the record, Boulder is home to America's first microbrewery (the appropriately named Boulder Beer) and is headquarters of the Brewers Association, while Fort Collins produces more craft beer than any other town in Colorado.

The quintessential day in Boulder starts with a hike in Chautauqua Park followed by a stroll down the Pearl Street Mall, stopping to watch the jugglers and buskers who hang out there, then lunch at an outdoor café (good even in winter). In Fort Collins, you bike along the Cache le Poudre River, pedaling past the giant New Belgium, Odell's, and Fort Collins breweries.

Boulder Information Center
13th St. and Pearl St., Boulder, 303-417-1365
bouldercoloradousa.com

Fort Collins Information Center
19 Old Town Square, Fort Collins, 970-232-3840
visitftcollins.com

● ●

VENTURE SOUTH
TO PIKES PEAK COUNTRY

In 1893, poet Katharine Lee Bates rode a mule to the top of Pikes Peak, where the scenery inspired her to write her famous poem, "America the Beautiful." Just an hour south of Denver, there are forty attractions all nestled in the shadow of the towering mountain. You can ride the world's highest cog railroad to the 14,114-foot summit, or drive up it. The thirteen-mile hike to the top of Pikes Peak is the highest vertical gain of any fourteener in Colorado.

Visit the chapel at the Air Force Academy (inspired by crossed swords), wander among towering red sandstone rock formations at Garden of the Gods, or walk through the underground world at the Cave of the Winds.

Stop at Manitou Springs for lunch. The Victorian town was at one time a major spa resort with a castle and several grand old inns. Today, it's a funky artisan community with street art, coffee shops, bars, and cowboy and mountain man stores.

Colorado Springs Information Center
515 S Cascade Ave., Colorado Springs, 719-635-7506
visitcos.com

FOLLOW
PIONEER HISTORY IN COLORADO'S FIRST CAPITAL CITY: GOLDEN

If Golden had been able to raise a little more cash in 1869, it might be the major city in the Rocky Mountains instead of Denver. Golden was the same size as Denver and back then was actually the capital of the territory. But while Denver boomed, Golden became a quiet mountain town in a spectacular location.

An archway over Main Street proclaims "Howdy Folks! Welcome to Golden." And they're not kidding. This is a friendly town with an Old West hospitality, mixed with a hot restaurant scene, the ultra-hip Golden Moon Distillery, and five breweries (including Coors, the world's largest). Golden is also an outdoor capital—bikes pedal up Lookout Mountain while hang gliders float down. There's a whitewater kayak park on Clear Creek right downtown and the USA Pro Challenge had the world's top cyclists racing along Main Street.

Golden Visitor Center
1010 Washington Ave., Golden, 303-279-3113
visitgolden.com

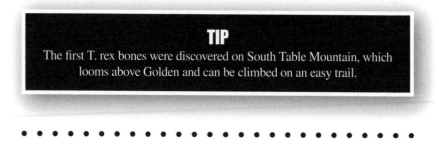

TIP
The first T. rex bones were discovered on South Table Mountain, which looms above Golden and can be climbed on an easy trail.

STROLL
THE PLANK-BOARD SIDEWALKS OF CENTRAL CITY

In 1859, this gold rush boomtown was known as "the richest square mile on Earth." John B. Stetson invented his famous cowboy hat here, Mark Twain visited, and Henry Stanley worked for the local paper before heading to Africa to find Dr. Livingstone. For sheer audacity, violence, saloons, and general craziness, Central City had no match. Then the gold played out and the fine brick-and-stone city became a ghost town.

The story might have ended there, but in the early 1990s, Colorado legalized gambling in Central City and neighboring Black Hawk. Now there are twenty-four casinos and more than ten thousand slot machines, poker and craps tables, and roulette, all going twenty-four hours a day. There's even a thirty-two-story Ameristar Casino Resort Spa sticking its head up high above the old mine shafts and pretty Victorian houses.

colorado.gov/centralcity

TIP
In summer, world-famous divas and tenors perform Verdi and Puccini in the acoustically perfect Central City Opera House, which was built by Welsh and Cornish miners in 1878.

124 Eureka St., 303-292-6500, centralcityopera.org

SKI WITH THE 10TH MOUNTAIN DIVISION
IN VAIL

During World War II, the army's 10th Mountain Division underwent high-altitude training on snow and skis in Colorado's mountains. In 1962, a group of these former soldiers opened a fledgling resort there and called it Vail.

Today, Vail is one of the largest year-round resorts in the world with 195 miles of ski trails served by thirty-one lifts that carry an astonishing sixty-two thousand people uphill an hour. The quaint, Bavarian-influenced main street is lined with hotels, shops, and restaurants. Stop for a bratwurst lunch at Hotel Gasthof Gramshammer, one of the originals. In summer, Vail hosts music and dance festivals. In winter, it becomes the epitome of a ski village with an ice-crusted river in the center and fairy-tale buildings covered in icicles and snow.

Vail Information Centers
Vail Village, 241 S Frontage Rd., Vail, 970-476-4790
Lionshead Welcome Center, 395 E Lionshead Circle, Vail, 970-479-4941
vail.com

TIP

To understand how this sheep meadow
became the most coveted resort of the rich
and famous—and to see vintage ski equipment
and posters—visit the Colorado Ski & Snowboard
Museum/Hall of Fame.

231 S Frontage Rd. East, Vail, 970-476-1876
skimuseum.net

WEAR HORNS
IN COLORADO'S BEST SKI TOWN: BRECKENRIDGE

Of course Aspen, Steamboat, Crested Butte, and Telluride might have a different opinion, but the best ski town in Colorado (within two hours of Denver) is Breckenridge. And "Breck" is most interesting in mid-January when thousands of people don Viking horns for the annual Ullr Fest—a parade with floats, frying-pan-tossing contests, and races honoring the Norse god of winter. Pronounced Oool-er, the Ullr Fest blends into the International Snow Sculpture Championships, in which teams of artists from around the world fill Breckenridge with twenty-foot-high, snow-carved masterpieces. At night they are illuminated, creating unbelievably beautiful illusions.

Founded in 1859, the old gold mining town is also one of the state's most historic. There are more than two hundred century-old buildings, most of them painted a rainbow mix of colors—purple, pink, orange, red, and yellow.

Breckenridge Information Center
203 S Main, Breckenridge, 877-864-0868
gobreck.com

TIP

Don't ski? Just down the road, Frisco has
a twelve-hundred-foot-long tubing hill, with
lift service to get you back to the
top for another ride.

616 Recreation Way, Frisco, 970-668-2588
townoffrisco.com

SCREAM
IN COLORADO'S ADRENALINE CAPITAL: IDAHO SPRINGS

Legend has it that the road from Central City to Idaho Springs got its name in 1868 when a terrified stage coach passenger sat in the backseat moaning, "Oh, my God, oh, my God!" at each turn. Today, the "Oh My God Road" (officially the Virginia Canyon Road) is still 8.6 miles of twisting and turning narrow dirt road, lined with cliffs with no guardrails. You can rent ATVs and travel up old mining roads and go horseback riding to century-old gold mines and cemeteries. Or you can hike on snow (even in summer) at spectacular St. Mary's Glacier. It's really just a permanent snowfield rather than a true glacier, but it can be slippery. Stay on the trails. River raft in Clear Creek's whitewater and zipline off a cliff.

Idaho Springs Visitor Center
2060 Miner St., Idaho Springs, 866-674-9237
clearcreekcounty.org

TIP

Hop into a hot bath at Indian Hot Springs,
where pure mineral water at 104 to 112 degrees flows
into geothermal caves, carved
out of solid rock in 1903.

302 Soda Creek Rd., Idaho Springs, 303-989-6666
indianhotsprings.com

SOAK UP THE VICTORIAN CHARM
IN GEORGETOWN

When John Denver was looking for the most picturesque town in Colorado for his holiday film, *The Christmas Gift*, he picked Georgetown. Ironically, millions of people zoom up I-70, never knowing that just a mile away there are two hundred Victorian buildings and one of America's most beautiful main streets. It was silver that made Georgetown rich and led to elaborate mansions and beautiful Victorian gingerbread homes. Admire the main street but walk the backstreets, past one colorful Victorian home after another. Stop to see the Hotel de Paris, one of the West's most opulent hotels. You could get French champagne and oysters here in the 1870s.

Georgetown Visitor Center
Exit 228 on I-70, 1491 Argentine, Georgetown, 303-569-2405
georgetown-colorado.org

TIP
Georgetown's annual Christmas Market has been held for more than fifty years over the first weekend in December, with outdoor fires, roasting chestnuts, outdoor food booths, and a visit from St. Nicholas in his traditional dress.

SUGGESTED
ITINERARIES

FOR THE HISTORY BUFF

DATE NIGHT

GET YOUR ART ON

FOR THE KIDDOS

GET HIGH IN THE ROCKY MOUNTAINS

ONLY IN DENVER

TASTE THE ROCKIES

ACTIVITIES
BY SEASON

FALL

WINTER

INDEX

The Broadmoor